D1560025

The Worker Question:

For Charles Mayne, S.J. who trusted
and Gerald Caine

The Worker Question

A new historical perspective on *Rerum Novarum*

John Molony

Gill and Macmillan

Published in Ireland by
Gill and Macmillan Ltd
Goldenbridge
Dublin 8
with associated companies in
Auckland, Delhi, Gaborone, Hamburg, Harare,
Hong Kong, Johannesburg, Kuala Lumpur, Lagos,
London, Manzini, Melbourne, Mexico City, Nairobi,
New York, Singapore, Tokyo

First published 1991 by Collins Dove, Melbourne
Designed by John Canty
Cover design by John Canty
Printed and Bound in Hong Kong

Contents

Acknowledgements

I wish to thank the archivists at the Archivio Segreto Vaticano and at Propaganda Fide, who were most helpful and courteous in their assistance to me. Also, Robert Barnes, Robyn Dutton, Bill Fox, John Merritt, Bede Nairn and Gerald Walsh who gave me valuable help and advice. I am grateful to the Australian National University for granting me study leave to work in Rome and to my colleagues in the History Department for their encouragement and friendship. Twenty-five years and seven books after starting with them, I now lay down the office but, hopefully, not the pen. They have been precious years, not the least because, from them, I have learned that history is truly a teacher of life.

Part I

Part 1

Introduction

Pope Leo XIII (1811-1903) issued an encyclical letter on 15 May 1891 entitled, in the Latin, *Rerum Novarum*, or 'of new things' in English. The document was quickly translated into many languages, of which English was one of the first, but it has always been known, and still is, by the first two words of its text, *Rerum Novarum*.

Encyclicals are letters addressed by the pope to the Catholic bishops throughout the world and through them to the whole Church. Frequently, they are also addressed to all those prepared to listen to their teaching, irrespective of religious adherence. In the last hundred years, the encyclical has become a common mode of papal teaching, because the increasing developments in the field of communications have made it more viable. Leo XIII wrote twelve important encyclicals on aspects of modern society, but *Rerum Novarum* has retained its foremost place among them.

Since 1870, there has been only one occasion on which a pope has defined a belief of the whole Church. It happened with the definition of the Assumption by Pius XII in 1950. In an encyclical, rather than setting down what the Catholic Church believes, a pope is more concerned to apply those beliefs to the world of the day in the religious, social, economic or political sphere. As such, an encyclical is the most important ordinary means of teaching that a pope has at his command.

By the 1880s, the fruits of both the French and Industrial Revolutions were apparent, especially in northern and western Europe, Britain and North America. The papacy itself had not remained immune from those effects, one of which, with the coming to fruition of Italian nationalism, was the loss of the Papal States. Pope Leo XIII had come to the papacy at a time when scarcely anyone expected that his would be a formidable voice in the shaping of the modern world. He was elderly, obscure and the occupant of a throne which, though more ancient than any other, scarcely seemed at odds with the affairs of the increasingly industrialised nations.

Nevertheless, in the Vatican there was considerable concern. In the nineteenth century, the essential factor that marked the relationship of the Catholic Church with those who for long centuries had been her children was the gradual loss of the workers in countries undergoing industrialisation. It was a loss which was most marked in the old Catholic countries of Europe, but not in those countries where the Irish clergy had maintained close ties with their people.

Other factors which agitated and perplexed the Vatican were the new economic and social relations brought about by the development of industrial capitalism. While there was an awareness that the loss of the working class was related to the new environment of capitalism, it was another matter to analyse what in capitalism was destructive of religion. That became evenmore difficult given the manifest fact that in northern Europe, in particular, many 'good' Catholics had embraced capitalism happily. How could such a development be accepted with equanimity when it was clear that interest rates often bordered upon usury, when the sufferings of the workers were so obvious and the imbalance of wealth grew daily?

Concurrently, democracy was everywhere more and more triumphant and nowhere more evidently so than in the New World. A Church which proclaimed the equality of all before God could only observe economic inequality with some degree of unease. Yet, if equality meant that all concepts of a hierarchical order were discarded in the secular sphere, perhaps it would not be long before the hierarchy of the Church itself was threatened. It was a matter that had to be treated delicately, and Leo had already done so in several of his previous encyclicals.

Since the days of Karl Marx, communism and socialism were other matters to perplex and concern the theologians. In particular, the long-held teaching on the inalienable right to private property seemed to be in jeopardy. At the beginning of his pontificate which lasted from 1878-1903, Leo was quick to assert the right of the individual to private property. His words fell on deaf ears among so many to whom such a right was little more than a dream when they observed the miserable chattels they called their own, and the impossibility, for the most part, of adding to them.

From the mid-1880s, there were calls for an encyclical by Catholic thinkers and bishops whose contact with the workers was sufficient to make them aware of the problem. Such matters as the role of the State, the conditions of work, the concept of a just wage and the organisational structures of the working class had been discussed, often with heat, in Catholic congresses in Europe. It was time, many thought, for the pope to put an end to discussion and come up with a blueprint on which Catholic social action could be based.

Few seemed to realise that it was utopian and injudicious to expect a definitive response from Leo. When Rome speaks, it has to be careful that short decades later it is not forced to eat its words. The 'new things' had not ceased to give way to even newer things. Capitalism was not an unchanging monolith. Modes of production, methods of distribution, and the economic theories which grew from the ordering of society under capitalism all underwent rapid change. Leo and those around him were not economists, ideologues or prophets. They could only stand on what they knew from the long tradition of the Church and apply its teachings to what they saw about them, or what they were told was the reality of the lives of the working masses.

In the event, the remarkable thing about *Rerum Novarum* was not that it was so late as some have asserted, nor that, in many areas, it remained on the level of general principles. That the encyclical saw with such clarity the problems of the working masses, confronted them with wisdom and generosity, and held out the hand of the Church to the workers was not remarkable. It was the responsibility of the Church to do so. More importantly, what the encyclical did was go to the core of the matter with its recognition that the new form of capitalism—in the eyes of the Vatican, a capitalism without Christ—caused chaos, greed, revolution, and great suffering among the masses. The encyclical is as much about capitalism as it is about the workers, but it also effectively criticises socialism which is a partial recognition that others also, theorists and activists, were struggling under capitalism and against its excesses. Nonetheless, to treat the encyclical as no more than a criticism of socialism is to deprive it of many of the positive and fruitful aspects it contains.

The vital thing for the encyclical was to break with the past. Leo was conscious that his predecessor, Pius IX, had condemned socialism, communism and liberalism, but his own task, while remaining firm on principles, was to go beyond condemnations and open a road to the future that would also be positive. Two things, in particular, from the past were still sources of great unease among European Catholics. The Church, for so long and in many countries had suffered from the intervention of the State in its affairs. The despoliation of Church property, the destruction of religious life by the appropriation of monasteries and convents, the forced military service of the clergy, the prohibition of episcopal statements, and a host of other irritants, and worse, had tended to make the State an enemy, rather than an ally, of the Church. Yet, there was a dawning realisation that, in the struggle for justice by the workers, the voice of the Church raised on their behalf was insufficient. *Rerum Novarum* took the important step of not merely recognising the need for State intervention. It positively encouraged it within carefully defined limits. That was a step of great significance.

The need for harmony among the different classes in society had long been a fundamental tenet of the Church. The question had arisen whether harmony would not be in greater jeopardy if workers combined in their own associations to deal with their employers. Would it not be better, many Catholic theorists said, that employers and workers should combine in mixed bodies where they could mutually thrash out their differences and work in harmony towards mutual goals? The alleged example of the medieval guilds was often put forward as a glowing aspect of a golden age, to which a return was desirable.

In the end, the encyclical, while recognising the example of the guilds, came down on the side of the right of the workers to join together in their own organisations. To the Catholic workers in the New World, long accustomed to membership in trade unions, there was nothing remarkable in this. In some parts of Europe, especially in places where Catholic employers had been wedded to capitalism, such a step was alarming. Once taken, however, it set the stage for Catholic worker organisations and eventually, for Christian Democratic parties. The political shape of Europe as it unfolds today owes much to *Rerum Novarum* because Leo was brave enough to turn to the workers, the masses of the people and give them a role in making the future.

The writing of a lapidary document does not happen quickly or easily. *Rerum Novarum* was no exception, and its gestation was long and painful. It was not in Leo's nature to turn to those outside his own papal household for help with an encyclical. Nor was he prepared to rely on the judgement or teaching of any one or other school of social thought, because he knew that, in so doing, the encyclical would immediately create divisions. Thus, *Rerum Novarum* was elaborated in an almost tortured fashion. Draft after draft was done in Italian and Latin and discarded. Month after month went by, and still Leo was not satisfied. He put his name to it in the end knowing that it was imperfect still, but yet it was the best that could be achieved in its time and place.

Rerum Novarum remains as a monument to Leo XIII, to those who inspired him to write it, and to those who collaborated with him in its evolution. Equally as important, is the fact that others listened to it and tried to build a new social order based on its principles. In the future, others again will turn to it when the question is asked why the Catholic Church still retains a voice and role in many of the most important affairs of the human race. The reason is simple. With *Rerum Novarum*, the Church,

The Worker Question

mindful of the Master to whom the poor and the suffering were
paramount, turned to them. Given the new role of the workers
under industrial capitalism, they could not be forgotten by the
Church. Without the workers, the Church, the State under
whatever form, and all human history have neither meaning nor
finality.

One

The Coming of New Things

The political and financial rulers of the advanced societies in continental Europe, the British Isles, North America and Australasia in the late nineteenth century were concerned about many new things. Principally, the fact that the workers were increasingly restless had become everywhere apparent. For decades, it had been possible to feed the workers a doctrine of passivity and acceptance, which would induce them to eke out their existence with resignation. Those days, it seemed, were over by the 1880s and, everywhere, the workers, through their organisations, were making claims to rights they considered were just, and demanding solutions to their problems.

The claims being made were simple and not extravagant, and they posed no necessary threat to the established order of society. The workers had one thing alone to offer—their toil. In return, they asked for the right to employment, to adequate remuneration for their labour, and for humane conditions in their work places. Individually, the workers possessed little power, but, collectively, their strength was immense. The fruits of their labour provided national security, economic wellbeing and an opening of the path to progress. Above all, labour helped to make possible the accumulation of capital which was the keystone of industrialised society. The withdrawal of labour would threaten to topple the whole edifice of capitalist society which the vast mass of the workers had no wish to destroy. To them, the civilising of capitalism would be sufficient. The question was how to achieve that goal.

Never since the neolithic revolution, which, long before the Christian dispensation, changed man from a food gatherer into a food producer and artisan, had the human race experienced such a discontinuity in the course of its development as that ushered in by the process of the so-called Industrial Revolution which began in the second half of the eighteenth century, first in Britain, then on the Continent, in the United States and Japan. Like every disruption in the course of history, the Industrial Revolution had widespread economic, cultural, social and political implications. It was based on the exploitation of inanimate sources of energy which gave rise to the factory system of production, the growth of industrial towns and regions and the creation of a new wage-earning class. Most importantly, in the course of a few generations, the whole process of the Industrial Revolution was accompanied by a spectacular increase in world population. The population of Europe, including European Russia, doubled to four hundred million between 1800 and 1900. The nineteenth century was hailed as the century of progress and prosperity, but there was a darker side to the material progress which was made in those years. It was revealed by the exploitation of labour by capital.

By the 1880s, murmurs of unrest had reached the ears of those who worked in the quiet corridors of the Vatican. The moment was singularly propitious because many of the great problems of the past were no longer of much concern. After 1870, the Roman question was a complicated matter of diplomatic negotiation because the Papal States had passed irrevocably into the hands of the new Kingdom of Italy. Since 1878, the new pope, Leo XIII, had continued to deplore the manner of the alienation of his States, turned fruitlessly to the Catholic powers for support and even gave consideration to leaving Rome. Before 1860, the pope had ruled a territory of 16,000 square miles, with three million inhabitants. That territory was now reduced to the few acres of the Vatican itself, where Leo chafed at his self-imposed seclusion. Nonetheless, a kind of working arrangement had been achieved under the law of guarantees of 1871 whereby the papacy and the Italian State were able to live together without constant violence or the threat of violence.

Leo thus enjoyed a freedom from worldly concerns which no pope had enjoyed for centuries. He could look at the problems which were disturbing the minds of rulers elsewhere and judge them with detachment. He had no working class dependent upon him except for a few servants and other workers in and about the Vatican itself, and the symbol of his tiara, with its triple division into spiritual, legislative, and temporal powers, had been rendered meaningless in its third element. Nevertheless, Leo's very impotency was his strength, because he could act towards the world as a father, rather than as a mere ruler among many other rulers. The weapon which remained to him was his word, and he was long accustomed to using it, whether in speech or with the pen.

The loss of the Papal States had engendered in the Catholic world a groundswell of sympathy for the 'Prisoner in the Vatican'. By the Catholic faithful, Leo was looked up to with pride and, among them, there was corresponding resentment against those in Italy responsible for his plight. It was possible for even the most humble to identify with Leo who seemed to reflect in his person the suffering of subject minorities everywhere.[1] Even the pictorial representations of the pope had become important. Upon Leo's succession to the papacy, his portrait was widely sought and displayed so that his physical appearance became known to millions who previously had thought of the pope as a remote and scarcely recognisable personage.

Furthermore, the development of the means of communication helped to foster those sentiments. It was now possible to have speedy and first-hand information on Vatican affairs through the Catholic press which was playing a significant role, even in English-speaking countries where its growth had been slower than in the Catholic parts of Europe. Peter's Pence (a voluntary contribution to the pope made by Catholics everywhere), which, through long ages had often been a cause of discord, had now become a fulcrum of unity as well as a means of showing solidarity with the pope. The Church in America, with its

9

strength in the working class in New York, Boston, Chicago and Philadelphia, had taken on a role of particular significance. American Catholics began to respond to the financial needs of the papacy, while American Church leaders extolled his person.

The most decisive step which had consolidated the position of the papacy in Catholic minds was the definition of papal infallibility by Pius IX at the first Vatican Council in 1870. The definition coincided with the final act of the loss of the Papal States and threw total emphasis on the role of the pope as pastor and teacher of all the faithful. Bishop Herbert Vaughan of Salford, England, summed up the prevailing sentiment in his report to Rome in 1879. The rolling cadences of his Latin lose nothing in English. 'The Roman Pontiff is the Pastor of all Pastors, the Infallible Teacher of faith and morals, the depository of the authority of Christ Himself, the centre of unity and the foundation stone upon which the Church of God is built.'

Vaughan went on to affirm with satisfaction that contributions to Peter's Pence had been tripled and he observed that 'the devotion of Christ's people towards the Holy See has been wonderfully increased'.[2] Italian liberals and freemasons, and others who thought like them, had fondly hoped that the loss of the Papal States would diminish the power of the papacy everywhere. They were already beginning to suffer disillusionment because the era of a modern and universal papacy had begun, and the fact that it was unfettered by temporal power had increased its moral strength immeasurably.

Leo was still a powerful prince, but he stood alone among those who ruled the European and other States. Like his predecessor, Pius IX, the new pope found small consolation from other rulers when he complained of the despoliation of his own States, and he was increasingly convinced that he could not look to the powerful for support. In the past, the popes had conducted their relations with hierarchies and rulers, while the masses of the people had stood in the shadows. Now Leo was being made aware that the masses were, in large measure, suffering under a new form of despotism in which princes counted for little because it was the economic system that affected all.

A simple pastor of West Cornforth, England, summed up his local situation to the Cardinal Prefect of Propaganda Fide in 1878. He said that iron foundries and coal mines were closing down with the result that there was 'neither work nor money for the poor'. [3] The same message of dependency on the capitalist system came from all quarters of the industrialised world. It was evident that, were Leo to seek an ally in the struggle that loomed ahead, he would not be found in palaces and in diplomatic circles. Any ally had to be sought in the new centres of power in the factories and workshops, and among the union leaders who were beginning to feel their strength in workers' organisations.

Leo himself was, in some measure, a man of the new age that had dawned. [4] Vincenzo Gioacchino Pecci was born in 1811 at Carpineto, near Siena, to a family of minor nobility, but of considerable means. His aptitude for serious study was quickly revealed at the Roman College where he was taught by the Jesuits, although his vocation to the priesthood was a matter of growth. It could be fairly said that young Pecci entered the Church as others in his time entered the civil service and, in his case, the two were synonymous. He was ordained priest at the age of twenty-six and was appointed civil governor of Benevento in the Papal States. In 1841, when he was thirty years old, he was sent to Spoleto and, later, to Perugia with the same role. In those positions, Pecci certainly achieved a degree of administrative competence but, more importantly, he was able to observe the daily lives of the people through the eyes of one who was primarily a civil servant rather than an ecclesiastic. He was a just and enlightened administrator who established schools and hospitals, reduced taxes, combated usury and promoted economic progress.

Moderation, common sense and strength of judgement were qualities that impressed the Vatican, and Pecci possessed all three in abundance, together with a measure of patience that stood him in good stead through the years. Six years from priest to archbishop was uncommonly swift, even for one close to high ecclesiastical circles, and at the age of thirty-two, Pecci, now archbishop, was sent to Brussels as Papal Nuncio. In Belgium, Pecci worked indefatigably for the restoration of Catholic intellectual life which had fallen to a low level, especially in the seminaries.

He also took the opportunity to attend, incognito, political gatherings of workers. As a result, his three years as Nuncio were generally well spent in that they enlarged his mental horizons. Pecci had come from the Papal States which had scarcely undergone any major change since the Middle Ages. Public education was in a miserable condition, industrialisation had made little headway, there were no railways (he had never seen a steam train until he arrived in Belgium), and social services were non-existent. In Belgium, the Nuncio saw the burgeoning capitalist system and the proliferation of factories giving rise to urban masses. He visited London and, generally, became aware of the reality of the changes sweeping over western Europe in the first half of the nineteenth century. For reasons which remain obscure, he was not acceptable to the Belgian bishops, and so he was recalled, but he returned to Italy much enlightened.

At Perugia, where he was appointed archbishop in 1846, Pecci was able to observe the beginnings of a united Italy. From his home on the edge of the Umbrian valley, he saw the promising first two years of the new pope Pio Nono (Pius IX), the revolutions of 1848, the occupation of Rome by Mazzini, Garibaldi and his troops, and the flight of Pio Nono to Gaeta in the Kingdom of Naples. The Pope returned to Rome in 1850, and the days of his co-operation in the building of a united Italy were over. He had finally understood that unity would mean the despoliation of the Papal States by men to whom anti-clericalism was endemic. He failed to measure the sweep of their longing for a united Italy and their determination to rid the Italian peninsula of foreign powers.

To Pio Nono, the makers of the new Italy were the implacable enemies of the Church and he wanted nothing to do with them. The twenty years between 1850 and 1870 saw the gradual whittling away of all papal temporal power and the final withdrawal of the pope into the Vatican. His last days were spent in bewilderment at a turn of events which had seen him come to the papacy in triumph and die in apparent defeat after a reign of thirty-two years on the throne of Peter—the longest in history.

Pecci retained a fine sense of balance throughout the thirty-two years he was forced to spend in a kind of exile in Perugia. He had been fortunate to incur the lasting displeasure of Cardinal Giacomo Antonelli (1806-1876), Secretary of State to Pio Nono as this effectively kept him free of involvement with Vatican politics during their most sterile phase. Pecci did not agree with many of Antonelli's political decisions and, especially, his implacable hatred of the Sardinian monarchy and of its despoliation of the Papal States. Nevertheless, as Archbishop of Perugia, he fought fearlessly against the agents of revolution in Umbria. Pio Nono finally elevated him to the College of Cardinals in 1853, but Pecci mostly passed his days in Perugia where he became an avid reader of international newspapers.

He was sometimes heard beyond his diocese by virtue of his pastoral letters which frequently touched courageously on the social question. In one pastoral letter, he spoke of labour as the 'first source of prosperity from which public and private wealth derives' and he wrote that the Church gave its support to labour, both intellectual and manual.[5] At the same time, there is no evidence that he gave much thought either to socialism or to the so-called 'spectre of communism' which, since Marx's Manifesto and the First International, appeared to propose the violent overthrow of the whole capitalist system as the fundamental solution to the workers' problems.

Although he was a cardinal, the Archbishop of Perugia was little known in Rome and, scarcely at all, outside Italy when Pio Nono died in 1878. His election was promoted within the College of Cardinals by a small group which included Cardinal Henry Edward Manning of Westminster. They were convinced that, with his love for Italy and his statesmanlike qualities, he would help to normalise the relations between the Holy See and the Italian State. Their lobbying was successful and, upon election on 20 February, Pecci took the name, Leo XIII. He had been an archbishop for thirty-five years and a cardinal for twenty-five, but he had made little impact on the Church. As an intellectual with a deep commitment to the teachings of Thomas Aquinas and a disposition towards the composition of Latin poetry, it was scarcely to be expected that, in his declining years, he would become an influential force.

Furthermore, his election took place during a period in history which to many seemed the nadir of the papacy. The Papal States were a thing of the past; capitalism, liberalism, freemasonry, socialism, and burgeoning democracy were the modes of the day and the papacy seemed, to some, an anachronism. After Leo's coronation as pope, a French Marquis who was present summed up the superficial thoughts of many by saying that it 'appeared to us as a shadowy likeness of vanished realities, as the exaltation of an illusion. We carried away from this ceremony the impression of a thing that was ending.'[6]

Leo XIII inherited two problems which seemed to overshadow all others, both of which were outwardly political and neither of which had anything much to do with the working masses. In Italy, no final solution seemed possible to the Roman question which had settled to restrained estrangement between the Vatican and the Quirinal (the Italian Civil Authority). In Germany, Bismarck was still in full flight with his attempt to subordinate the Church to his will and make it Prussian rather than Catholic. They were, nonetheless, problems which could be expected to exercise fully the mind of the new pope. Yet there were other voices urging Leo to turn to the problems of the workers and, with time, they could not be gainsaid.

The social question, with its fundamental problem of the relationship between labour and capital, had been slow to come to the serious attention of Catholic thinkers. Since the thirteenth century, some theologians, including Thomas Aquinas, had come close to the core of the matter. Aquinas wrote on both labour and wages and saw labour as principally directed towards the acquisition of the necessities of life. This consideration, however, did not lead him to formulate the proposition that a just wage needed to include an element which would permit the worker to provide for those dependent upon him. The Dominican Archbishop of Florence, Antoninus (1389-1459), developed the idea further and said that a wage had to include an element which would cover the needs of those dependent upon the worker, but the idea was not sufficiently formulated to gain widespread acceptance as a requirement in justice.

Martin of Abypilceuta explicitly stated that it was unjust to pay a wage which was not in proportion to the work done. In his opinion, if an unjust wage were forced upon a worker, or if he accepted it out of ignorance, the contract between employer and employee lacked validity and the employee was entitled to seek recompense and take what he rightly deserved by using other means. By the seventeenth century, the concept of a just wage and the need for it to contain an element to provide for the family of the worker was clearly taught by the Spanish Franciscan theologican, Il Corduba who was followed closely by Vasquez and De Lugo.[7]

These, and similar propositions, excited little attention because they were enunciated in a period when both custom and public opinion saw a necessary link between a wage and the provision of the means of livelihood for the worker and his family. The link was cut by the entry into the workforce of vast numbers of women and children consequent upon the Industrial Revolution, the emphasis on the profit motive, and the doctrine of laissez-faire that had begun to prevail, and which left the price of labour to be determined by market forces. Furthermore, the Napoleonic Wars and the disruption they caused in European society, the change in the power balance in Europe and the emergence of England and, later, the United States as world economic powers had thrown emphasis on new, democratic forms of political organisation in society and away from the basis of the old social order.

At the invitation of Pio Nono, Father Giocchino Ventura preached a sermon in Rome on 28 June 1847 to honour the memory of Daniel O'Connell. During the course of the sermon, Ventura said that the Church would christianise democracy and would say to it, 'reign and it will reign'. There was an immediate and alarmed outcry from conservative elements in Rome, but the pope ordered that the sermon be published exactly as it had been given, remarking, 'I think like the author.'[8] When he was driven from Rome by revolutionaries purporting to be working in the name of the people, Pio Nono probably regretted his remark. Nevertheless, democracy was increasingly the new form of the modern state and it had to be accepted as the coming reality of political organisation. By Leo's time, there were some Vatican prelates who accepted this fact, including Leo himself who, when Archbishop of Perugia, had been a close friend of Ventura.

Outside the Vatican, there were other prelates, especially in the English-speaking countries, to whom democracy was not merely acceptable, but was seen as the most Christian form of the state. The other fact that was apparent to them was the existence of toiling masses to whom the shape of the State was of little moment because they existed under iron economic laws which governed their whole lives. In the past, the content of Christian thought had been shaped by crises that were christological, ecclesiastical or intellectual, but the late nineteenth century forced the so-called social question to the fore. Some, understandably, saw it as an essentially political question which it certainly became when solutions were proposed. Others tried to deal with it on a doctrinal level knowing that, without a solid base in theory, political solutions would run the risk of sterility, mere posturing and transience.

In Rome itself, Leo XIII was closely associated with three Italian-born cardinals, Simeoni, Franchi and Rampolla, each of whom had served in international posts. Mariano Rampolla del

Tindaro had been Papal Nuncio in Spain and became Leo's Secretary of State in 1887. A Sicilian, educated in Rome, Rampolla was of such gifts and distinction that he would have succeeded Leo to the Papacy in 1903 had his candidature not been vetoed by Austria, to whose interests he was alleged to be hostile. His years with Leo were decisive for the development of Vatican attitudes, not least to the social question, and his was a major influence in shaping the pontificate which he served loyally.[9]

Nevertheless, from the beginning of his pontificate, Leo himself was aware of the social question. He condemned the errors of socialism with their denial both of authority and the right to private ownership of property, and he encouraged the formation of worker societies, under the guardianship of religion, in his second encyclical, *Quod Apostolici Muneris*, dated 28 December 1878.[10] He strove to give a solid theological and philosophical basis to modern Catholicism with his plea for the revival of a thorough knowledge of the thought of Thomas Aquinas. In his encyclical, *Aeterni Patris*, dated 4 August 1879, he made it plain that, by restoring the cathedral of Thomistic thought, he was not calling for a retreat to the medieval past. Leo's main objective was to reject the idea that faith and reason were irreconcilable. Furthermore, it was to Aquinas that he looked for the principles which would buttress a lasting social order in which justice would prevail.[11]

It was not, however, from his immediate circle that the primary impetus came which motivated Leo to turn his attention to the factories and workshops, to the people who owned them and to the workers who toiled within them while suffering under the iron laws of a system that seemed impossible to reform. Despite the work of the Italian Movimento Opera dei Congressi and its paternalistic concern for the workers, it was difficult for Leo to learn much on the social question in Italy where industrialisation was still in its formative years and where there were, consequently, few Italians conversant with its full implications. Such was not the case in some other European countries, especially Germany, France and Belgium, while England, which had given industrialisation to the world, was long accustomed to its development and use, as was the United States.

In Germany, Franz von Baader, professor of Philosophy at Munich since 1826 and, formerly, a foundry manager in England was forthright in his denunciation of 'the abyss of the physical and moral misery of the Proletariat' which he had observed at close quarters. He condemned the Manchester school of liberalism and called for the formation of trade unions as the unique means which would restore the workers to their rightful place in society.[12] Von Baader was followed by Franz Joseph Ritter von Buss who was elected to the Lantag of Baden in Freiburg in 1837. He proved to be an outspoken champion of the workers by calling for restrictions on working hours for children, fourteen hours as a limit for adults, safety regulations in factories and a health insurance scheme, partly financed by employers. He proved too far ahead of his time to be given serious attention.[13]

The role of the episcopate as the pivotal force in Catholicism was firmly established in the nineteenth century and it is not surprising that three bishops became the principal contributors to Catholic ideas on the social question and to the development of a Catholic social movement. They were: Ketteler at Mainz, Mermillod in Geneva and Manning in London. In a sense, they were unlikely sources from which the impetus towards a reshaping of Catholic social theory would flow because their connection with the world of the workers was tenuous. Nonetheless, their largeness of spirit, keenness of intellect and, above all, their dedication to the cause of the poor and the dispossessed, whom they saw embodied in the working class, admirably fitted them to be the standard bearers of new thought.

Wilhelm Emmanual von Ketteler (1811-1877) took a degree in law and became a member of the Prussian public service in 1835, and it was to him that Alcide De Gasperi looked as a fundamental source on the elaboration of a Catholic response to the social question in the nineteenth century in Europe. Indeed, Leo himself called Ketteler 'our great predecessor' and said, 'it is from him that I have learnt'.[14]

After the arrest of the Archbishop of Cologne by the State authorities for his lack of compliance on matters dealing with marriage laws, Ketteler resigned from the public service, studied for the priesthood, and was ordained in 1844. He was elected to the Frankfurt Parliament in 1848 and became Bishop of Mainz two years later. He was forced to turn his energies away from public life as his diocese had fallen into a lamentable state during the reigns of his two immediate predecessors. Prior to his appointment to the episcopate, Ketteler had already become a public figure due to the interest aroused by his Advent sermons on the social question which he gave in the Mainz cathedral in late 1848. In them he proclaimed that the social question was the great problem of the age, and he devoted much of the rest of his life to its solution.

Industrialisation in Germany developed slowly in the early years of Ketteler's episcopate and he was slow to formulate other than theoretical concepts. They were firmly based on the basic notion of the natural law, especially as enunciated by Aquinas, and he held that governments were bound to follow its prescriptions. But he took up a firm position in relation to the laissez-faire liberalism of the Manchester school which, he said, had produced a slave market in Europe where the workers, like animals, were mute victims. To him 'Manchester Liberalism was merely a form of State absolutism masquerading under liberal phraseology administered by a bourgeoisie whose guiding ideal was that of rampant egoism.'[15]

Ketteler saw the right relationship between the State and society as one stemming from the principle of subsidiarity. It was a simple concept which held that the component elements of society such as individuals, the family, associations, and co-operatives should exercise their own rights and duties, while the communal elements on a broader scale, including the State itself, should only step in when the common good demanded intervention, or the weaker elements were unable to exercise their rights.

Although initially attracted to co-operatives as a means to alleviate the plight of the workers, the bishop soon realised that, by themselves, co-operatives lacked the power to bring about radical change. In his great work, *Die Arbeiterfrage und das Christentum*, published in 1864, Ketteler castigated the capitalist system which regulated wages merely by supply and demand, leaving the price of labour, and consequently, the wellbeing and, even survival, of families, at the whim of changing economic forces. While close to Marx in his awareness of the alienation of the worker from his labour, Ketteler did not go as far as Marx who also saw alienation existing in pre-capitalist society. Like his Catholic contemporaries, Ketteler regarded medieval society as that most closely resembling a Christian ideal, although he did not call for its reconstruction because he realised that the past could never be repeated.

Ketteler's most decisive mental step was to recognise that both the State, through intervention, and the workers, through association, were, in combination, the only effective means of solving the worker question, which was how the social question had come to be defined. He soon began to defend the right of the workers to better conditions and to higher wages. He also affirmed the right of the workers to strike, which he regarded as the principal weapon of the trade unions in their struggle with large industry and capital. At the Fulda Bishops Conference in 1869 he stated, without equivocation, that the State was bound to intervene in the economy and conditions of the workplace. He saw this as essential in order to bring to German society a degree of humanisation as the prelude to its christianisation. To him, capitalism seemed bent on the dehumanisation of society.

Ketteler was probably little heard outside his immediate circle, but his voice helped to develop a climate in which it became acceptable for bishops to pass judgement on the social question. When Ketteler's book was republished for the fourth time in 1890, Ludwig Windthorst claimed that the bishop's ideas had been solemnly recognised by the young Emperor, William II. De Gasperi caustically wrote, 'Exactly twenty-six years later! With the war of 1870, the Kulturkampf and Bismarck in between!'[16]

Cardinal Mermillod spent ten years in exile from his diocese of Geneva between 1873-83 and, finally, was able to return when Leo cut the ground from under Bismarck by conciliation and the Kulturkampf was over.[17] Since 1872, Mermillod had been called 'the bishop of the social question', but he, too, lacked the opportunity or the feel for the practical application of his thought. He was responsible for the presentation of a petition at the Vatican Council which called for a clear enunciation of the principles of social justice, especially as they applied to the problems of the working class. The Council was unable to continue its work after September 1870 when Italian troops occupied Rome, although Leo often thought of reconvening it. But the seed was sown, in that Mermillod had looked to the highest forum of the pope in council for the taking up of a position on the social question.

Mermillod's most important contribution, however, was a deep conviction that socialism could not be opposed simply by prohibition or by merely deploring its excesses. Mermillod realised that it was necessary to go to the workers, to have confidence in them and to love them, while using all the remedies proposed by economic thought to help them. But, in some measure, it was too late, because the European working masses were ill-disposed to listen to voices which had for so long preached resignation. Many of them had begun to hear other voices wherein rang the often strident, but also siren, tones of revolution and radical change. The calm voice of Mermillod found it hard to get a hearing in that cacophony.

Henry Edward Manning, convert to the Catholic Church from the Anglican ministry, Archbishop of Westminster since 1865, and Cardinal since 1875, had never lacked a sense of the importance of the social question.[18] In 1874, he formulated his ideas publicly at a conference in the Mechanics Institute at

Leeds which was published as *The Dignity and the Rights of Labour*. Manning's fundamental argument was that, when the rights of the workers were not respected by the employers, and when the workers were unable to defend themselves, the State was bound to intervene. It was a courageous stand to take at a time when there were powerful voices in both Church and State saying that intervention was a worse evil than the situation it proposed to remedy. Manning clearly saw that phrases such as 'free contract' and 'the independence of adult labour' were pure cant, designed to ensure that the workers remained isolated and devoid of the strength that unity would bring or the protection a concerned State could proffer. To him, it was a self-evident truth that 'between a capitalist and a working man there can be no true freedom of contract'. Capital always remained 'invulnerable' provided the worker continued to give of his labour.

Manning knew that dire poverty was widespread in Britain, which prided itself as being the richest nation on earth. The plight of the workers troubled him deeply, although he was aware that the dreadful conditions of fifty years previously had been mitigated by State intervention through Factory Acts and inspection of workplaces. Nevertheless, Britain had not acted to raise the minimum age of child labour even to twelve years. Manning was also aware that children working as 'half-timers' and women on shortened hours were being exploited by employers who saw them as cheap labour.

Manning's concern for the dignity of women was central because he saw the very fabric of society threatened by their exploitation. He wrote that the spectres of the 'chain-makers of Cradley Heath, the pit-brow women of the mines and the mothers in our factories rise before us'. When the great dock strike of 1890 dragged on relentlessly, Manning finally and successfully intervened. He scorned the voices of the employers who said that the strike was 'a matter between us and our men'. The Cardinal reminded the employers 'that there were two other interested parties between masters and men, the multitude of women and children, and the whole peaceful population of

London'. Although he was aged, feeble, and in the last years of his life, Manning's voice was a powerful incentive urging others to act. To Manning the time was ripe for Leo to speak, 'for never till now has the world of labour been so consciously united, so dependent upon the will of the rich, so exposed to the fluctuations of adversity and to the vicissitudes of trade'.[19]

Manning was not the only Catholic prelate in England who proclaimed the rights of the workers. Bishop Edward Bagshawe of Nottingham was well known for his writings and his activities in the same area although Manning, while acknowledging the goodness of the Bishop, regarded him as 'imprudent, obstinate, impetuous, and lacking a sense of conciliation' which became publicly manifest when Bagshawe condemned a secret society called the Primrose League in 1886.[20]

The result was that Manning was reluctant to rely on him as an ally, although Bagshawe took a strong stand at the Catholic Congress in Liège, Belgium, in 1890. State intervention in the social question was the principal theme around which the congress revolved. Many continental Catholics had a deeply ingrained suspicion of the State which sometimes bordered on hysteria. Their suspicion was understandable given their long and unhappy experience of the regimes in Belgium, Germany and France where the Church had suffered repression.

Manning was unable to go to the congress, but he sent a letter which, when read, caused a sensation. Its most significant passage alarmed many. 'I do not believe that it will ever be possible to establish peaceful relations between owners and workers in a useful and lasting manner until a just, fixed and publicly established regulation is recognised that determines profits and wages; a measure upon the basis of which all free contracts between capital and labour will be governed.' This caused a Belgian parliamentarian of conservative views to respond, 'I fear the State and I hate Caesarism.' In reply, Bagshawe argued strongly and sensibly that the State retained its right to intervene even if it was sometimes the case that it overstepped the mark. He cited his knowledge of London, where thousands of workers toiled for seventeen hours daily, six days a week, yet were unable to earn enough from their labour to live by it. In Bagshawe's view the State alone could remedy such an evil, but the congress timidly called for an international convention to limit working hours.[21]

Scarcely any other Catholic voice in England was heard in Rome on the social question. The Bishops were limited in the reports which they submitted at five-year intervals to the Roman Congregation for the Propagation of the Faith. They were expected to follow a set formula by answering a series of questions which gave them no scope to touch on social matters, except in response to questions 51 and 52, where they were asked to comment on abuses against faith and morals. Apart from an abiding concern with so-called 'secret societies', in which the Romans had an interest, given the involvement of freemasonry in the loss of the Papal States in Italy, the bishops were mainly troubled by the prevalence of drunkenness, especially among the Irish, and mixed marriages between Catholics and Protestants. Even Manning was moved to set up a Catholic League of the Cross which bound its members to total abstinence because he thought that 'no sin or vice amongst the people has its source other than in this fountain'. Bishop Richard Lacy, of Middlesborough was alarmed at drunkenness, but noted that, 'on Sundays and Feast days the poor in great numbers are bound to go to work. Furthermore, it is customary for employers to pay their workers in pubs (camponibus), from which it is frequently the case that they emerge drunk.'[22]

The Bishop of Portsmouth, John Virtue, was uneasy about Manning's League of the Cross. To him, some drunkards, once they joined the League, became entangled in the tentacles of Scylla while trying to avoid Charybdis because, once reformed, they tended to become proud of their new found sobriety and often joined the Fenians and promoted hatred of authority.[23]

The aged Ullathorne, last survivor of the Vicar Apostolics before the days when Pio Nono restored the English hierarchy in 1850, went to the heart of the matter. He had known the Irish from long before when he had worked as a young Benedictine in Australia in the 1830s. Later, he had met them in their thousands in Birmingham where he was their pastor and bishop. Ullathorne wrote that the Irish and their descendants in England were leading precarious lives.

> *They do the hardest, most humble and least remunerative work. The girls and women work in factories, the men rarely ever become skilled workers. Amongst the upper classes and the proud they are often despised and covered with shame; they are treated as aliens in England. For the most part they live in miserable localities separated from the English and they pay a weekly rent for shabby and almost empty rooms . . . Frequently they are improvident, spending their wages in taverns, not so much because of a love of drink but in order to find comfort in the enjoyment of the company of each other.*[24]

It was a fitting note on which Ullathorne ended his long episcopate because it was his last report to Rome.

In other ways, however, it was an appropriate moment for Leo to speak to the Catholics in England. Leo celebrated his golden jubilee of priesthood in 1887 and the event fostered such support for his cause and veneration for his person that it was taken by some to inordinate lengths. From London, a certain Mr Rupert Graham wrote to tell the pope that he had named his two sons Leo Ludovico and Vincenzo Gioacchino Leo. Tracy Turnerelli of the same city composed a hymn which he claimed was being sung in many schools. One verse ran:

> *Leo! Father! Pontiff-King!*
> *Imprisoned as thou art, thou still*
> *Art strongest of Earth's Kings*
> *And nations, listening to thy voice,*
> *Obey the call it brings.*

This choice piece of doggerel was accompanied by a letter accusing Propaganda of incivility in not thanking him for a previous communication. Pencilled on the letter, in Italian, were the words, 'more moans and insolence', leaving it unclear whether Cardinal Simeoni, to whom the letter was addressed, referred to the poetry or the other sentiments expressed by Turnerelli.[25]

In a much more serious vein, Bishop Herbert Vaughan reported that he had distributed to his faithful one thousand copies of Leo's encyclical *On the Christian Constitution of States (Immortale Dei)*, which had come out in 1885. He said that it was the only 'sound and Catholic teaching on the matter' although what his people made of the elevated and complicated tone of the document was not recorded. Edmund Knight, Bishop of Shrewsbury, was worried about nationalism and socialism and regarded 'liberalism as the true fountain of all false principles'. He too, was convinced that it was time for the pope to address himself to matters of serious moment, especially for the sake of the clergy, although he was unsure what they were and even less sure as to whether the pope would be taken heed of by his audience.[26]

Possibly, the letter from England that most interested the Romans in those years came from Bernard O'Reilly, Bishop of Liverpool.[27] It awakened all the bitter memories of 1849, the occupation of Rome by the Mazzinian revolutionaries, the flight of Pio Nono from his city and the final steps leading to the loss of the Papal States. O'Reilly wrote to say that an old man lay ill in Liverpool, paralysed, dejected in spirit and full of sorrow for the sins of the past. The penitent had two particularly grave sins on his conscience, at least in the eyes of the Roman Curia. On Easter Sunday, 1849, he, Emiliano Luigi Spola, priest, Doctor of Law and former official of the Sacred Congregation had been so much inflamed by the rhetoric of Mazzini that he had usurped the papal place.

Spola had said Mass at the high altar in St Peter's and emerged afterwards onto the loggia of the church to bless the people, which was a solemn act reserved to the pope alone. When Pio Nono returned to Rome, Spola had fled to England from where he now pleaded for the absolution which only Leo could grant. The absolution was speedily given, but in those years since 1849 no white-clad figure had appeared on Easter Sunday to bless the people, the city and the world. Leo lived for a quarter of a century without ever leaving the Vatican and, in the papal chambers, the Roman question remained a problem to which constant attention was still given.

Two

Awakening of Consciousness

Despite the awakening of consciousness that had begun to take place in some parts of Europe and the British Isles, when Alcide De Gasperi asked himself in later years where the new Christian social movement was born, he vacillated only temporarily and opted for Austria, although he recognised that France also had some claim to priority. In his opinion, Austria offered the 'most favourable social and political climate for the birth and the cultivation of those reforming ideas which are more particularly known as "Christian-social"'. Furthermore, in his judgement, the 'most logical, most radical and most systematic' master of the Austrian group was Baron Karl von Vogelsang.[1]

De Gasperi was singularly placed to make a judgement on such matters when he came to reflect on them in the 1920s. He had studied at the University of Vienna from 1900 to 1905 and became the youngest member in the Austrian Parliament in 1911. Furthermore, he had an intimate knowledge of the events and of some of the principal actors in the Austrian social movement in the nineteenth century. As a result, he looked to Austria, and Vienna in particular, as the formative nucleus of the new developments in Catholic circles. The ideas formulated there passed on to France through the pages of *Association Catholique* which was published in Paris. That nucleus finally gave birth to the common Austrian-French school which, blending with the Swiss school, was given a concerted shape by the Union of Fribourg which was seen subsequently by others as the seedbed of *Rerum Novarum*.[2]

It was in Vienna, in 1875, that Baron Karl von Vogelsang came into contact with the publication of the Austrian federalists, *Der Vaterland* and, from that moment, the idea of a

Christian social-reform movement was given a voice. Vogelsang had a Prussian military, aristocratic and Protestant background which was an unlikely field for the development of progressive thought.[3] However, he became convinced of an idea that lay at the heart of the new reform movement and within which also lay the fatal seeds of its own divisiveness. He decided that civilisation, as he knew it, was the unique product of Catholic Christianity in the medieval period and that only from that source would the ideas and movements spring which would defend and restore civilisation.

The temptation to confuse the material with the spiritual and the transient with the permanent tended to elevate and make fundamental some aspects of the Christian past, especially the guilds of the Middle Ages, and thus give them a role well beyond any true and lasting value that they might have possessed. Such a conviction, furthermore, made the Church a civilising force with vast implications for the nature of her salvific mission. It ran the risk of making the Church an instrument to be used in the manner of Constantine and Charlemagne; whose example was not lost on Mussolini in a later period. Finally, it was an easy step from seeing the Church as the unique matrix of the good, true and just to judge all ideas and movements as flawed or invalid that did not spring from the same origin, that did not fully express its ideals, or were in partial disagreement with it.

After his conversion to the Church in 1850, Vogelsang moved gradually to the centre of Austrian Catholic life by residing in Vienna and being entrusted with the editorship of *Vaterland*. In that role, he developed and disseminated his ideas on the reform of society and of the economic system itself. In 1890, the socialist paper *Arbeiter Zeitung*, summed up the kernel of his thought in a way which Vogelsang would have accepted as valid. He had recognised that the existing social order was divided into horizontal classes. He wanted to see a vertical division based on professions, in which owners and workers would be united in bodies called corporations. The corporations would express externally their common interests, while their conflicts would be peacefully resolved internally. The socialist paper said that such utopianism would result in the abolition of classes and the demise of class warfare.

Such a solution may have been utopian but scarcely less so than that posed by the socialists to the perceived reality of class conflict. They wanted struggle, if need be, violent struggle, to wipe away the capitalist State and usher in a classless society. To Vogelsang, the same end could be achieved by harmonious means. He saw the rigid reality of class divisions in Austria based on the three tiers of nobility, industry and peasants. To him, society had its own independent existence and the State was the creation of society by which it maintained order and administered justice. The State was bound to reflect the shape of the society which gave it birth, thus the parliamentary system, through the corporations, had to represent the respective classes of society and their interests.

Among those European Catholics who feared State intervention, especially State socialism, many saw in these ideas the embodiment of their fears. They feared, rightly, that the corporations would express the interests of the powerful. They also feared that, were the State made up of corporations through their representation in the parliamentary system, the result would be a State that was no longer servant and instrument, but master and wielder of society's destiny.

Vogelsang believed firmly that man was a creature of God, rather than a product of inexorable brutish and chaotic forces which shaped him and his destiny. Man, enlightened by divine teaching as expressed by the Church's magisterium and strengthened by grace, could master the forces of nature and shape them to his own end. It was said that the feudal society of the Middle Ages had been constructed on that basis and, in Vogelsang's view, the highest values of Western society had sprung from it. The individual thrust for wealth, as epitomised in his own society, revolted him. He wrote, 'the Germanic Christian social order, itself the most noble flower of the human spirit, was the product of the long and difficult work of the

Church on our fertile soil. It knew nothing of property, but only the use of the common good.'[4]

It did not take Vogelsang long to conclude that the very basis of rampant individualism, given concrete and organised shape in capitalism, was the lending of money at interest which to him, was usury. The old Prussian aristocrat, still aflame with the fervour of his conversion to the Church, rejected the arguments of theologians who attempted to justify usury. Their reason was that the lender put his capital at risk, which became especially the case when the enterprise of the borrower failed and the capital could not be paid back. To Vogelsang, usury always remained intrinsically evil. If the ancient Fathers of the Church had found good reasons to condemn usury, reasons which were still cogent at the Fifth Lateran Council in the early sixteenth century and had convinced Benedict XIV in the eighteenth century, they still held good for Vogelsang.

He was not prepared to admit that economic circumstances had changed in that, in the past, capital itself was non-productive and therefore the lender, when paid back in full, had received all that was due to him. Modern theologians argued that capital had become productive which meant that the lender, through interest, was entitled to share in the productivity of the capital he loaned. Such matters were as nothing to Vogelsang who saw usury as the basis of that very society which had replaced his beloved feudalism. Capitalism was triumphant and from it many evils flowed.

Finally, an answer to the problem of the mode of production had to be sought which was not a mere repetition of that proposed so widely though socialisation. Socialisation was no solution because it would remove even further any real involvement of the worker from the fruits of his labour. Again Vogelsang's approach was simplicity itself. 'The solution to the worker question, which will give justice to the working class, cannot be other than by the disappearance of the working class and its absorption into the owner class.'[5] How this was to be done remained unclear. Vogelsang realised that leaving it to the generosity of the owners was utopian, while doing it by State intervention was to create the very Moloch State he feared. To him, it was not a matter of abolishing private property, nor of putting labour under State control, or of passing the distribution of the fruits of labour to the State. He saw it realised through the freeing of productive property from its privatisation which would result in it being set free 'from the egoism of the single individual'.[6]

Vogelsang clearly envisaged that the reform of the whole world of work would be achieved by the harmonious development of the corporations which were to be the keystone of the whole edifice. In order to set them up, a political party in power had to take up Vogelsang's programme as its own platform. The German Centre Party, through its long struggle during the Kulturkampf had partially exhausted its energies and, more importantly, it strove to come to terms with the reality of the modern State. Windthorst, its leader, had an ingrained suspicion of anything that smacked of a return to the past, no matter how ideal or how seemingly in accordance with the highest Catholic traditions it might have been. Vogelsang could not have been optimistic about getting much of a hearing in those quarters.

The Germans did, however, take up the worker question on a practical level and, as early as 1877, there were moves towards legislation in the fields of factory conditions, the prohibition of children's work and the limitation of that done by women, obligatory apprenticeships, and other remedial steps. Such proposals were received with alarm by the liberals who could only concentrate on their idea of freedom, which meant in practice freedom to exploit the workers further. In any case, the ideals of the Centre were eviscerated by Bismarck who, afraid of the rising tide of socialism, began himself the partial amelioration of the conditions of the workers by means of insurance in times of sickness, unemployment and old age.

With their power as a reforming force muted, the theoreticians of the Centre began to argue amicably over Vogelsang's ideas and, especially, over corporations. Some favoured the idea, while others treated it warily. They said that if corporations worked at all well in the Middle Ages, it was only for a brief period of perhaps two hundred years and then only when they relied absolutely on the good will of the owner class. If the State was not an abstract concept, but an amalgam made up of human beings, there were disturbing examples of its behaviour at hand and were the corporations to rely on the State for their existence they might well be in peril.

One only had to look at the Iron Chancellor himself to recall how the State could behave when an individual, or a group of individuals, decided to use it for their best interests or, even worse, when they used it in the interest of that other abstraction born of the Reformation and called the Nation. Would the State be free of such tendencies even were it made up of benevolent corporations was the question which no one could answer? Such ideas were never put so bluntly but the long and bitter experience of State intervention in the affairs of both the Church and society, for which the State, in Burckhardt's words is 'only a protective shield', was always there as a constant warning.[7]

The question of usury and its effects on the shape of modern society was an even thornier problem. It was one thing to claim that Vogelsang was a man of the past, dreaming of a society in which good reigned triumphant; it was another to deny the manifest evils of human misery and economic enslavement that sprang from unrestrained, industrial capitalism. It could certainly be claimed that capitalism also did much good because the genuine human needs of many millions could only be met by the more efficient modes of production which only capitalism seemed capable of offering at the time. Vogelsang said that the black heart of capitalism had to be gradually drained by the progressive abolition of usury.

What would then replace capitalism was unclear except some form of medieval paradise which no one could readily accept as viable. An alternative was certainly offered by socialism, but Leo had already made his mind clear on that subject in his encyclical, *Quod Apostolici Muneris* of 1878, in which he had said, 'the socialists wrongly assume the right of property to be a mere human invention, repugnant to the natural equality between men, and, preaching the community of goods, declare that no one should endure poverty meekly, and that all may with impunity seize upon the possessions and usurp the rights of the wealthy'.[8]

Given the atheism of Proudhon, the blatant materialism of Marx and Bakunin and the constant attacks on the Church which continental socialism mounted, it was unlikely that any Catholic would have dared contemplate a socialist solution to the social question. Consequently, some form of compromise with capitalism had, perforce, to be found. Nevertheless, there were passages written under divine inspiration which seemed to indicate that the common possession of goods was an early response to the teachings of Jesus and the apostolic Church at Jerusalem 'held all things in common, and would sell their possessions and goods and distribute them among all according as anyone need'. (Acts 11: 45) The Desert Fathers and the monastic communities in both the East and West had given an example over many centuries of a form of socialised economic and human behaviour.

Yet Leo had not found it possible to discern any good in socialism because an examination of its tenets, on which very few socialists themselves could agree, revealed it as fundamentally flawed by its materialism. It is not surprising that no one spoke of the need to baptise socialism and weave within it the precepts of the Gospels, except for the small band of Christian socialists in England who failed in their efforts, apart from their influence on the co-operative movement.

With a good deal of vigour, Leo deplored the excesses of socialists in their anxiety to destroy, so as to rebuild. With their proclamation of 'monstrous views' which attacked all forms of authority, their utterances on the family and their impracticable desire to deny all right to property, the pioneers of the socialist movement had strained every effort to alienate all sympathy from orthodox Christian sources. Leo's language was unrestrained in his condemnation. 'We are alluding to that sect of men who, under the motley and all but barbarous terms and titles of Socialists, Communists, and Nihilists, are spread abroad through the world and, bound intimately together in baleful alliance, no longer look for strong support in secret meetings held in darksome places, but, standing forth openly and boldly in the light of day, strive to carry out the purpose, long resolved upon, of uprooting the foundations of civilised society at large.'[9]

The Catholics of the German Centre Party needed no special directive to reject Vogelsang's programme of destroying capitalism by cutting off its life blood. They did it by saying that the shape of capitalism, based on the development of technology and on the rational use of capital, was a fact of life. They regarded it as a development which showed the progress human beings were making towards more perfect expressions of social cohesion. At the time, they could only faintly see that capitalism, in its unrestrained forms was awash with unfettered individualism, the love of mammon, the unbridled and seemingly insatiable lust for profits, and the flooding of markets with products which often took little account of the true needs of people, and, especially, those of the poor. Nonetheless, it is understandable that the prevailing view was that capitalism had to be accepted, although its excesses were deplored.

The task of the Church was to come to the aid of those who sought to 'civilise' rather than destroy capitalism, but it was an uneasy alliance because the Church could never shake off her vision of the poor and the oppressed on the one hand, nor her allegiance to another Master on the other. As a result, capitalism would never be free from criticism. Meanwhile, socialism withered in the embrace of sectaries and ideologues where it never, or rarely, encountered the infusing power of regenerative Christianity. When its shape was finally revealed, socialism proved that the spirit was the true creator of the shape, in that force became its motive power, and materialism its base.

To Leo and those close to him, such as Rampolla, the older nations of Europe were still the major preoccupation in the

Vatican. They were close to home, relations with them had gone on for centuries, and the records of those relations were carefully filed in the Archivo Segreto. Although their problems were vexatious, it was almost a matter of affairs within the family which could be dealt with in traditional ways. Across the Alps lay France, first daughter of the Church peopled by those whom Leo, castigating the more excessive anti-clerical acts of the fledgling Third Republic, called that 'most noble race of Gauls'. But there was some uncertainty as to whether the filial piety of that 'first daughter' could continue to be relied upon.

In Germany, the full rage of the Kulturkampf was muted by 1887 and the young Kaiser, William II, gave promise of wanting closer association with Rome while looking to the Catholic Centre Party to support him in all things in return. By March 1890, Bismarck was gone, Windthorst, long the valiant, principled, but pragmatic leader of the Centre was old and dying, and who could tell what the future held for the Church in the Second Reich? The spectre of socialism had taken flesh in the Reichstag with the election of twelve socialist deputies in 1887 and the number had risen to thirty-five in 1890. The question was soon, and necessarily, put whether the new, self-proclaimed representatives of the working class were to become the anti-clericals of the last decade of the century and draw the workers with them in another attempt to suppress or control the Church.

In any case, the growth of international socialism, the increasing use of the strike as a weapon and the way in which the workers seemed to be helping to make relevant the concept of class warfare all proved that the old order was passing. In Austria, Switzerland, Belgium and Holland there were problems, some as old as the centuries while others were new, but the nations of Europe all stood at Leo's doorstep and he could scarcely fail to hear what was being said among them, especially on the new question of socialism.

In France, the impetus for change since the developments caused by the French and Industrial Revolutions was apparent and a few French scholars, who belonged to the group which published the review, *Association Catholique*, were engrossed by the problems which change had brought about. They engaged in theoretical discussions on the desirable shape of a Christian France, the worth of the Revolution as compared to the *ancien régime*, the right to property, agrarian reform, and such matters. The most important example of a working model on which a new society could be shaped was the Christian Corporation of Val-des-Bois, founded in the Rheims region by the industrialist, Leon Harmel in the early 1870s. Harmel was motivated by the need to cut through all posturings and dispense with theoretical ideas in an attempt to solve the workers' problem in a practical way. The development of harmonious relationships was the key to his idea and, to this end, he set up a mixed corporation of owners and workers which had various sub-groups to deal with pensions, health, savings, and the like. In this way, the owners, bosses and workers came together for clearly defined ends. The major body, a Directive Council, as well as its subdivisions, was always presided over by an owner.[10]

Harmel's corporation, as an experiment, was admirable despite the reality of its paternalism. Yet it afforded no more than an isolated and unique instance of a successful attempt at harmony, although it was justly famed in its day and visited by such people as Cardinal Gibbons. There was one notable aspect of its constitution which did not attract much attention but which had its origins in the conviction of the great social reformer, Frederick Le Play, that without freedom there could be no progress. Harmel had come under the influence of Le Play and he was anti State-intervention and could not countenance the idea that corporations should be set up by the State. In accordance with this idea, membership of his corporation was entirely voluntary and, in fact, some of his workers chose not to join.

It was precisely on the question of State intervention, or on an enlargement of it, that differences arose in France, much as they had in Germany. Indeed, a fear of intervention by the State in the affairs of the individual was more keenly felt there, and with reason, than in Germany. Two members of the French nobility, the Marquis La Tour du Pin and Count Albert de Mun were leading figures in the Catholic social movement. De Mun was a man of the Right who regarded the Compte de Chambord (known among his followers as Henry V) as the legitimate King of France. He also felt that the logical fruits of the French Revolution were found in socialism and, consequently, he pronounced himself an irreconcilable counter-revolutionary.

Albert de Mun had sufficient magnanimity, however, to recognise that some changes had to be made in society and, as he mourned over the burned walls of the Tuilleries in mid-November, 1871, a worker friend said a few words to him that changed the course of his life. 'Who is responsible if it isn't you the rich, the great ones, the enjoyers of life who pass the people by without looking at them or trying to uplift them.'[11] From then on, de Mun threw himself into the work of the *Association Catholique*, helped with the development of workers' clubs and, together with La Tour du Pin, was converted to the corporate ideal when he saw its practical expression in Harmel's Corporation in 1873.

De Mun entered parliament as a Catholic royalist in 1880 while La Tour du Pin went to Vienna as military attaché from 1879 to 1881. There he met the upholders of the feudal world represented by *Vaterland* and his own strongly conservative ideas were given added strength. To him, and to those who thought like him, the past had more value than the present. The medieval period was hallowed with the marvels of the ancient guilds and the divine right of kings and, if it could be recreated, a new age would dawn for Europe and the Church. It was essentially a romantic and nostalgic view of the past with little basis in historical fact, but its appeal lay in the sense of well-being and comfort to be imparted by the harmony of a hierarchical devolution of power from God to king to subject. Such a view had no relationship with the existing order based on capitalism and democracy and it was bound to sink into oblivion.

Once he returned home, La Tour du Pin joined forces with de Mun and others connected with *Association Catholique*. To them, the only way to restore French society to something like a proper order was to have the State make the setting up of mixed corporations of owners and workers compulsory. In that way, a kind of corporate regime would be established which, in the future, would itself become the State. The outcome would be the restoration of the Christian State based on the medieval, feudal pattern. With their rejection of the fruits of the French Revolution they had failed to see that, with all its tawdry sloganising, the infant form of democracy they saw about them was preferable to what had preceded it. Indeed, they failed to see that a corporate State would be a sham democracy with power in the hands of a few who would ensure 'harmonious' development by suppressing deviation.[12]

Other influential French Catholics did not accept any State intervention beyond mere recognition of the corporations. Count Breda; the Louvain professor, Charles Perrin; Claude Jannet, professor of political economy at the Catholic Institute in Paris; the Jesuits of the powerful review *Études*; and the Catholic owners' association of northern France at Lille, all intuitively saw the danger of the corporate regime based on State intervention and they rejected it. Indeed, in respect of the corporations and their medieval precursors, the guilds, Perrin said, 'The guilds had their day of greatness and prosperity in the Middle Ages; and to attempt to revive them now . . . would be to engage in an impossible struggle against the deepest convictions of the society of our own day.'[13]

At the Catholic Congress of Liège, in 1890, it was their voice that prevailed and the concept of a corporate regime, dear to La Tour du Pin, de Mun and Vogelsang was laid to rest even to the extent that, in its conclusions, the congress refused to use the word corporations and adopted the term, 'professional organisations' instead. It refused to vote on a motion which proposed that a committee be set up to study the corporative organisation of society. The State was called upon to recognise, protect, but not enforce, professional organisations, and there the matter rested. It was among the French, therefore, that the theoretical battle was fought which finally made it clear that the ideal of a corporate regime was not Catholic, but one which rested upon a concept of a monarchical and hierarchically ordered medieval society. Such a society was entombed with its relics in the royal mausoleums of Europe.[14]

The French were active as well on another fruitful level. In 1885, and, again on the occasion of the pope's golden jubilee of priesthood in 1887, French worker and employers' groups went to Rome on pilgrimage. The fact that they came to Rome was important, but more significantly was the manner in which Leo received them and the way in which he made it abundantly plain that he wanted to hear directly from the world of the working class. In 1885, Leo exhorted them to revive those ancient institutions called guilds, which, in better times, were born and flourished under the imprimatur of the Church. He thus gave further impetus to La Tour du Pin and de Mun and revealed that, by the mid-eighties, little thought of a constructive nature had been given to the social question in the Vatican.

Nevertheless, in the Vatican, situated in Italy and staffed predominantly by Italians, there was some genuine response to local conditions. Although Italy, by the 1880s, was still largely unindustrialised, some beginning had been made and, by 1881, there were six thousand metal workers, mostly in the North, but a workers' movement based on large industry was scarcely apparent. Furthermore, the old socialist movement which drew its inspiration from Bakunin did not take a Marxist shape until 1880 so that in the preceding years it could be dismissed as an odd phenomenon of little influence. The whole political and economic thrust of the young Italian State was directed at laying the infrastructure of development, largely bureaucratic, and the struggle for power was conducted in an arena, and on a level, far removed from preoccupations with the workers' problems, which if they did manifest themselves by violence, were quickly repressed by the State.[15]

The Church, insofar as it was represented in the new State by its lay members, was by its own choice, marginalised by the decision called *Non expedit* of 1867 which meant that Catholics could not be either electors or elected. One outlet for enthusiasm was through manifestations of solidarity both within and without Italy in which Catholics expressed their sympathy with the pope and their determination to see a satisfactory solution to the Roman question. Indeed, the Catholic movement in Italy from its early days through to the mid-1880s was partly a set-piece orchestrated from the Vatican to protest at the loss of the Papal States and at the equivocal position in which the pope found himself.

The director of this operation was the secretary of Propaganda Fide, Monsignor (later Cardinal) Dominico Jacobini. The so-called pilgrimage for Leo's jubilee in October 1881 was an example of how the system worked. Priests were sent through the Italian dioceses to get support, articles on the Roman question were published in *Osservatore Romano* with the expectation that they would be reproduced in Catholic papers, even in France and Germany, and it was further expected that considerable sums of money would be raised to meet the legitimate and extensive needs of the Holy See. Giovanni Aquaderni was the layman in charge of the movement and he was responsible to Jacobini who he bluntly told to give up his position or do it properly. He said to Jacobini that, if the Vatican wanted the Catholic movement, it was necessary 'to give it the importance it merited and to support it with the means used in the nineteenth century, a century of journalism, steam and the telegraph, otherwise it is better to suppress it . . .'[16]

A typical response to the 1881 pilgrimage was from Lodi in the form of a telegram which read, 'The Catholics of Lodi with the parochial groups of the city will be united in spirit tomorrow with the Italian pilgrims praying at the feet of the crucifix with St Mary Magdalen to repair the insults launched against Your Holiness and Your Glorious Predecessor Pius the Ninth.'[17] Leo was both elderly and practical and it is unlikely that such encomiums brought him any comfort or light. It is little wonder that the French, highly organised and led by men of the calibre of Harmel, were welcomed warmly by Leo.

Despite the preoccupation with matters which a few forward-looking thinkers regarded as museum pieces, it would be unjust to see the work of the Italian Catholic movement, inspired by the old papalists Salviati and Paganuzzi, as no more than an emotive and reactionary expression of largely sterile protest against the new State of Italy. It had other and much more fruitful levels of existence which, in their own way, helped to form a climate of support for more profound developments on the social question. Since 1874, the *Opera dei Congressi* had brought together numerous organisations in Italian Catholic society, co-operatives, banks, newspapers, representatives of the rural workers and the like, and gradually, questions of moment such as wages and conditions were discussed. In fact the *Opera* had a section which passed from being entitled simply 'Charity' to 'Charity and a Catholic economy' and finally to 'Christian social economy'. As early as 1877, at the Congress held in Bergamo, a motion was passed which wanted to see worker's organisations recognised as having a legal right to exist and, in principle, to be allowed representation in the deliberate assembly of the State. Motions were passed on children under twelve being employed in factories and a plea was made that children and women should not work more than a nine-hour day while at Lucca, in 1887, the Congress turned to the weighty matter of wages and the prevailing low levels paid by employers.[18]

Especially because the Italians were more removed from the turmoil and anguish which had begun to convulse the workers' movement in the more industrialised countries, they were able to bring a greater sense of detachment to their discussions and study and let others weave their way through the maze of thorny problems that the other societies had to face. Leo himself had given considerable impetus to both clarity and calmness in theoretical matters by his support for a return to the teachings of Thomas Aquinas whose example in the *Summa theologiae* was one of prudence and precision.

Some few of those who recalled the days when he was Archbishop of Perugia possibly also remembered the pastoral letter he wrote for Lent in 1877 which had the title 'Civilisation and Religion' in which he addressed himself to the sufferings of the industrialised workers. 'With what great sorrow do we hear that, even in countries that are judged as the very pinnacle of civilisation, he who has to earn his bread with the sweat of his brow has excessive hours of labour imposed on him. And the sight of the poor children who are sent into the factories to be debilitated by premature labour surely saddens the Christian observer and draws words of fire from every generous soul. Do such things not oblige governments and parliaments to frame laws to put a stop to this inhuman traffic?' He went on to ask whether 'these supporters of a civilisation which is outside the Church and without God, instead of helping us to progress do not push us back centuries to a time when slavery crushed such a large part of mankind and the poet Juvenal exclaimed that the human race lived as the plaything of the few?'[19]

Given the alleged propensity of Italian Catholics to backwardness, it may be surprising that when Ketteler's ideas on corporations were first known in Italy, they met an immediate and sceptical response from the Catholic economist, Fedele Lampertico, despite the fact that positive mention was made of them at the congress at Lucca in 1887 and a call was made for their re-creation. Lampertico derided the notion that the guilds, in Italy at least, were a fine flower of the Middle Ages. As far as he was concerned the guilds fell apart, not because they were demolished by fanatical revolutionaries, but because their very nature contained the seeds of their destruction in that they denied any true freedom to their members. Lampertico cited how a shoemaker could be accused of a 'crime' because he patched his son's shoes rather than sending them to a cobbler.[20]

Lampertico's great pupil and colleague, Guiseppe Toniolo, took a larger view and, especially in relation to Tuscany where, in the Middle Ages, he saw the fundamental principle in operation of personal liberty growing out of the freedom of intermediary organisations. To him, that was a vast improvement on the preceding structures of a Roman state with a workforce held in slavery.[21] Toniolo had the greatest effect of all contemporary thinkers on the Italian movement and even in his early days he tended to regard freedom from State intervention and freedom of association as the principal characteristics of any future trade union or corporative movement. In 1871, in the days of Pio Nino, an association was formed in Rome of artists and their associated workers which had the mutual aid and education of its members as its principal aim. Its fortunes fluctuated, but its very existence in Rome was a reminder of happier days when the Church and the workers tried to meet in an atmosphere of mutual esteem, rather than hostility. Toniolo approved of this practical expression of co-operation and, at the same time, worked through the 1870s and 1880s at a theoretical expression of the Catholic attitude to the social question.

Although Luigi Sturzo thought that Toniolo retained an essentially medieval view of the world, the fact remains that, unlike Vogelsang, Toniolo accepted the shape of the modern economic order which he asserted had to be transformed rather than destroyed. The agents of transformation would be Catholics who accepted the teachings of the Church on mankind, society and the State and who would work through intermediary bodies to bring about change.

By the late 1880s, however, much remained to be clarified, both in regard to the defining of principles as well as gaining an understanding of the actual state of affairs in the social order. No one was at all sure what the Vatican had to say on the question of principle and the matter of intermediary bodies remained in limbo. Were they to be trade unions in which the workers organised themselves for their own purposes or were they to be corporations of owners and workers? In either case, what was the role of the State, if any, in their foundation and later operation?

From the time of unification a rural workforce had begun to emerge throughout Italy consonant with the transition from a semi-feudal economy to a capitalist one. High taxation, lack of communications in the form of railways and good roads, lack of capital except that in the hands of the large landowners and the banks, and the need to mechanise had resulted in an increasing number of the Italian peasantry losing their ties to the land and becoming reliant on wages. In industry there was still widespread artisan and domestic production, but gradually, throughout the north, an industrial base was developing which was most notable in industries based on food production as well as on textiles, such as silk, cotton and wool. Thus, in the years before 1890 there was a change from old forms of production to capitalist ones based on wage labourers, so that the problems which had become evident in northern Europe were developing there also. The result was that the *Opera dei Congressi* began increasingly to deal with the social question manifested in the world of the workers.

In the years 1882 and 1883, a small group of Catholic noblemen and clerics met in Rome. The Austrian, Count Kuefstein, Count Blome, Monsignor Jacobini and Father Denifle, SJ, discussed such matters as rights to property, work, and loans at interest, which were questions Vogelsang and his associates in Vienna were thrashing out at the same time. Clearly, the Roman group lacked any practical experience as it included no one with a first-hand knowledge of either industry or of the workers' movement, nor was there any economist of note among them. It is scarcely surprising that nothing new or theoretically constructive came from such deliberations.[22]

The important thing was that, in Rome, there were men trusted by the Vatican to whom the social question was not unknown. Another overlapping group also came together, allegedly at Leo's suggestion, but neither group had any direct role in the immediate formulation of *Rerum Novarum*. It met in the home of Prince Paolo Borghese and included Jacobini, Benucci, Santucci, Soderini, Talamo and Denifle. Only a few fragments in written form came from its deliberations, but two books of considerable importance were published. The first was by Father Burri which dealt at length with the concept of a just wage. The other scholar who certainly made up part of the Roman group was the Jesuit, Matteo Liberatore. He was born at Salerno in 1810, became a scholar and theorist of some standing, and a writer over many years in the Jesuit magazine founded at Naples in 1850, *La Civiltà Cattolica*. In 1889, Liberatore's *Principii di economia politica* was published in Rome and, intellectually at least, the stage was set for Leo, himself, to speak of the social question.[23]

Another lever which moved Leo to decide that an encyclical was needed on the social question was the emotional impetus engendered by the French pilgrimages to Rome in 1885, 1887 and 1889. In 1885, only industrialists and organisers were present and Leo said to Harmel who was leading the group, 'The next time bring the workers to me also.' In 1887, two thousand workers were present carrying hundreds of banners and representing twenty-one different groups. Leo surrounded himself with all the pomp of his Roman court, including sixteen cardinals who listened to speeches by Langenieux and De Mun. It was not possible for De Mun to relinquish the dream of the past and he said:

> *We are the representatives of the first workers' corporations which have been reborn at the appeal of Your Holiness in order to protect, under the guidance of religion, the interests of the world of work and the way of life of the workers themselves.*

When Leo spoke he, too, harked back to a glorious past:

*In the days when its voice was better heard and obeyed by
the faithful . . . the Church came to the aid of the poor and
the workers, not only by its works of charity but by creating
and encouraging those great corporate associations, which
have contributed so potently to the progress of the arts and
trades and procured for the workers themselves much that is
of great value, as well as a greater degree of wellbeing.*

In asking the workers to recognise the role the Church had
played in public life in the past, Leo was careful to limit the
participation of any interventionist body in the future and in
particular the State. To him, State intervention in the social
question was not necessary in the absolute sense because when
'morality, justice, human dignity and the domestic life of the
workers' were not offended there was no need for the State to
play a direct role in workers' organisations. However, when the
above values were menaced or compromised, States had the
obligation to intervene so as 'to protect and defend the true
interests of their citizens'.[24]

On 20 October 1889, a pilgrimage of ten thousand workers
from all the provinces of France, led again by Harmel, listened to
Leo. On this occasion he began to adopt the magisterial tones of
a universal pastor,

*To those in positions of power We say — you must have the
heart and compassion of a father for those who earn their
bread by the sweat of their brow . . . You must accept the
truth that, in order to remove the dangers threatening
society, neither repression nor military means will suffice.*[25]

In a sense, Leo was already beginning to anticipate the major
outlines of basic papal teaching on the social question. It was
becoming increasingly clear that the time was ripe to speak,
because others were already taking the initiative. The idea of
holding an international conference on the worker question had
been bandied about for some years, but had come to nothing. In

1886, the Union of Fribourg had asked the pope to call such a conference and, in 1887, Gaspare Decurtins, a leading Swiss Catholic, had a similar proposal passed by the Swiss Federal Council. Leo was pleased, but before any action was possible, the Germans had decided to take the initiative so that, when Kaiser William II called the Berlin conference in 1890, Leo was able to do little more than send a letter of adhesion and encouragement to him although the Kasier said that Leo had 'always used his influence in favour of the poor and forsaken of human society'. Still, however, Rome remained silent, despite the memorandum placed before Leo by the Union of Fribourg in February, 1888. It concluded:

> *Everyone is now looking to the Vatican for a word . . . If your word will make itself heard in the world and put in high relief the dignity of work and the value of its rights, if it will call together the workers into Christian associations, they will not become the prey of the enemies of Christ but they will be the most faithful champions of the freedom of the Church.*[26]

Whatever else, the voice from the Vatican was not going to be raised in unseeming haste. Leo and those about him knew that they could not act in the manner of Marx and Engels and issue a manifesto to the workers which their successors, if not their contemporaries, would look upon with regret. Their prudence was a source of strength because they refused to lay down lines of action which were not based on long-held principles. Leo could only speak in carefully modulated and fatherly tones which the impetuous would perhaps reject as too weak. Nevertheless, in the end, it was not to be clamour, but sense, which would endure.

Three

Voices from America

Despite the genuine and deep concern of the Catholic intelligentsia, the tragedy for continental Catholicism was that, already, the working masses had been in large measure alienated from the Church. Too often, it had become the case that, in the industrialised cities, the grinding hours of labour had weakened the hearts and bodies of the workers so that religion had become a luxury, rather than the essence of the spirit. Too often, again, it had seemed to the workers and their leaders that the Church either stood removed from their plight or, even worse, that the Church had taken the side of their masters. Dispirited, worn down by their labours and their anxious care for the needs of daily existence, the workers were mostly passive, but some saw direct action through the trade unions, or the burgeoning socialist parties as the only remedy for their miserable condition. Marx and Engels had published their *Communist Manifesto* in 1848 with its comforting promise that the 'proletariat' were certain to be triumphant in the long run, and the first volume of *Das Kapital* had come out in 1867. Undeniably, the ideas of Marx were partially a reaction to the problems of industrialised Europe, but the Church had been slow to reply, other than on the level of denunciation.

In the United States, Canada, Australia, New Zealand and in those parts of Britain where the Irish, in large numbers, went to seek an existence, the clergy had remained close to their people. For the most part, the bishops and priests were Irish or the sons of Irish immigrants. They had grown up in poverty, they had struggled to obtain an education and they had seen the effects of that struggle on their families. They were able to observe at first-hand the condition of the workers, but above all, the priests knew by name the people among whom they had grown up and then served as pastors. They saw to it that the Catholic working masses were not lost to the Church.

Unlike the situation on the continent where those who proposed remedies for the workers were mostly removed from the world of work, in the English-speaking world, it was unusual for reactions to the social question to find any deep theoretical elaboration. The development of trade unions and trade union congresses, which formulated practical solutions and demanded their adoption in legislation and their acceptance by capital, was the norm. The gradual realisation that formal worker representation in parliaments was needed if long-term political action was to be effective gave rise to political parties and the Australian Labor Party, founded in the 1890s, although having its origins much earlier, was the clearest example. Albert Métin, a French visitor to Australia, summed up his attitude of wonderment about the lack of theoretical formulations by writing a book, *Le Socialisme sans Doctrine*. In it, he quoted an Australian worker who he asked to summarise his programme. The reply was: 'My programme? Ten Bob a Day!' However, Métin recognised that pragmatism had some value when he admitted that, while the Australian and New Zealand worker movements had not formulated theories, they had gone 'infinitely further than any other country in the practical field'.[1]

Nonetheless, there was one American theoretician, Henry George, whose writings were of particular interest in the Vatican and whose ideas had a decisive effect on the timing of *Rerum Novarum* and, to some degree, on its contents. George was born in Philadelphia on 2 September 1839 and was reared in an atmosphere deeply imbued with puritanism. Before his marriage to an Australian in 1861, he became a Methodist and remained a committed Christian for life. Widely travelled, he settled to regular employment as editor of the San Francisco *Times* in 1866. The social question gradually attracted his interest and, by 1871, he was arguing against the private ownership of land. The publication of *Progress and Poverty* in 1879, followed by *Social*

Problems in 1883, brought him a measure of international fame as a social reformer of some minor consequence.

The simplicity of his ideas, none of which was original, won him a following. George never espoused socialism, indeed he eloquently opposed it, but his doctrine of a single tax held considerable appeal for many of those who were concerned about the evident fact that, as wealth increased for the few, poverty likewise became the lot of many. The single tax proposed by George would permit the State to take a one hundred per cent return from unimproved land values. Such a step, according to George, would lead to the eventual abolition of other taxes, the removal of the State from most areas of public life, and the resolution of the conflict between capital and labour.[2]

It was comparatively easy to deride George's views as extreme, puerile, or even insane, but it was another thing to combat them effectively. The reason was that George believed sincerely, and taught persuasively, both with pen and word, that the social question demanded a ready and radical solution. Not surprisingly, the fervour of his followers was matched by the sense of urgency and resolution with which they espoused and propagated his doctrines. 'The key to the success of George's adherents . . . lay primarily in that crusading spirit of dedicated individuals, the almost religious devotion of the Single Taxers to a belief in their panacea. The zeal of these converts, the intellectual climate at a time of great industrial strife and economic depression, the messianic appearance of Henry George, "Hero, sage and prophet" . . .' combined to make George's name a household word on countless lips in the English-speaking world.[3] In the Vatican, not much interest was shown in George until its attention was drawn to the fact that one of his main followers in America was the pastor of New York's most important parish, St Stephen's. He was Father Edward McGlynn.

McGlynn was a former student of the College of Propaganda Fide in Rome. The Congregation of Propaganda Fide, which ran the College, never ceased to take a benevolent interest in the later careers of its students, although such benevolence was apt to be mitigated if any student erred in his ways, especially if he showed any tendency to depart from unswerving devotion and loyalty to the teachings of the Holy See. McGlynn, however, began his career with marked distinction and became a superior at the newly founded American College in Rome, before returning to his home diocese, New York, in 1865.

At St Stephen's he quickly achieved local fame as a priest with very decided views. He urged his people to receive daily communion which, before such a devotion was espoused by Pius X thirty or so years later, was regarded as extreme. He refused to build a Catholic school and held that education was the province and duty of the State so that he urged parents to send their children to public schools. In the eyes of his Archbishop, Patrick Corrigan, McGlynn's apparent financial incompetence was an even greater cause for concern. By the mid-1880s he had run up a debt of $145,691-69c, and he was accused of an annual expenditure on flowers of $5,000 which, even in the wealthy parish of St Stephen's, was regarded as an unwarranted luxury.[4]

The blackest mark against McGlynn, however, was that he had begun to espouse with fervour the ideas of Henry George. At a public function to mark the departure of the Irish patriot, Michael Davitt for home in 1882, McGlynn went as far as to state that an absolute title to land was 'contrary to the ends of justice', and that 'the doctrine which holds that everyone has an equal right to land cannot be condemned by the Church.' George had been even more explicit in *Progress and Poverty* and his words were taken careful note of in Rome. 'The poorest child born today in London has the same rights to the hereditary lands of the Duke of Westminster as his eldest son has.'[5] The Italian government had recently indicated that it also had similar ideas, at least in regard to the right of the Pope to an absolute title to his States. It was unlikely that, in the Vatican, the ideas of George and McGlynn would be looked upon with favour.

Throughout the 1880s, considerable attention was paid to George and McGlynn by the Vatican authorities, and Archbishop Corrigan provided ammunition from New York on both of them. McGlynn was alleged to have said that, unless the Church wanted to continue to preach resignation to the poor it was necessary 'to read and study *Progress and Poverty* and there you will find the only true and adequate remedy for the evils of modern society'.[6] George had visited Manning in London and had, allegedly, been told by the old Cardinal that there was nothing in his book that warranted condemnation, while the bishops of Clonfert and Meath in Ireland had approved of every word it contained. Manning later denied having ever read the work, although he conceded that George seemed to him to be modest, thoughtful and calm, but he confirmed that he had read *Social Problems* and found nothing offensive in it.[7]

Archbishop Corrigan tried to stem the tide of enthusiasm created by George and McGlynn by writing a Pastoral Letter in which he used Leo's encyclical *Quod Apostolici Muneris* on Socialism (1878) to defend the doctrine of an individual, inalienable right to private property, but to no avail. It was easy for Corrigan to dispose of George as a socialist with 'mad' ideas, but McGlynn was a popular and much admired pastor whom he pursued relentlessly. He accused the priest of being pro-Fenian, in favour of violent revolution in Ireland and, in his refusal to bend to ecclesiastical authority, was supported by 'Fenians, Socialists and Members of Secret Societies.'[8]

The American affair was assuming proportions beyond its importance because McGlynn had offended both his Archbishop and the Propaganda authorities by his apparent disloyalty. The situation was made more difficult because, exactly at this time, both in the Vatican and, generally, in the English-speaking world, but especially in Ireland with the Fenians, the matter of so-called secret societies had caused considerable unease. The memory in the Vatican of masonic involvement in the loss of the Papal States was very real and the existence of such societies anywhere with Catholic membership was a cause of grave concern.

In America, the organisation most under scrutiny was the Knights of Labour. Founded in 1869, they were little more than a mutual aid society for workers although they followed a semi-masonic ritual. Nevertheless, with the fever of distrust of secret societies and Leo's own personal animus against freemasonary they were bound to raise suspicion.[9] In his *Humanum Genus* (1884), Leo saw all the main evils of modern society such as communism, socialism and nationalism as stemming from freemasonry, and the loss of the Papal States involving Mazzini, Young Italy and assorted societies merely went to prove the point.

A Catholic mayor of New York, Terence V. Powerdly, had become Grand Master of the Knights of Labour in 1878 and the fact that he was a fervent supporter of both George and McGlynn only tended to cloud the issue further, as had McGlynn's public support for Powerdly when he ran for mayoral office. The matter of the Knights became serious, with some American bishops such as Corrigan insisting that they be condemned *tout court*. For the time being, saner views prevailed, and in August 1881, the Holy Office agreed to refrain from condemnation, provided the Knights removed words savouring of socialism and communism from their constitution and made it plain that everyone had a right to acquire a portion of the earth which God had given to the human race.[10] Powerdly was able to accept these restrictions, but McGlynn was proving immutable in Corrigan's attempt to bring him into line.

While action on the Knights required prudence, the McGlynn case was seen as something that could be settled peremptorily. On 4 December 1886, the Pope insisted that McGlynn appear in Rome to explain himself, which McGlynn promptly refused to do. He had become even more forthright in his attitudes and, in refusing to go to Rome, he wrote to Corrigan to say that he would always teach that 'land is legitimately the property of the people in general and its private ownership is contrary to natural justice, irrespective of any civil or ecclesiastical law by which it is upheld'. He went further and said that, had he the power, he would change all laws and confiscate individual ownership 'without a penny's recompense to the so-called owners'.[11]

By January 1887, Leo was more insistent that McGlynn come to Rome and, in the event that he did not do so, he was to be suspended from the exercise of his priestly duties. Corrigan, aware of what had transpired, became even more agitated and wrote to Leo to say that 'the poison of Henry George's doctrines spreads daily . . . even Protestants wonder at the delay in your judgement' and implored him to act 'for the dignity of the Holy See'.[12]

In the meantime, some bishops in the United States had become aware of what was afoot in Rome. It was clear that, not only were George and McGlynn under scrutiny, but so also were the Knights of Labour. The most senior of the bishops, Cardinal James Gibbon of Baltimore, was visiting Rome and, as he was not Roman educated, he felt freer in his dealings with the Vatican than men such as Corrigan whose whole ecclesiastical education had been undertaken there. On 20 February, 1887, having ascertained the lie of the land in Rome, he sent a lengthy document to Cardinal Simeoni at Propaganda Fide.[13]

The document began with an attack on monopolies, but Gibbons, aware that there were some who were calling for the revival of guilds as an antidote to monopoly capitalism, insisted that there was no place in America for institutions which smacked of the medieval past. In regard to the workers, he agreed that strikes could sometimes be violent, but he asked that those who condemned them should also look at the provocation which caused them. To Gibbons, real power was now in the hands of the people and not in those of either parliaments or princes which, as Manning had pointed out, made it imperative for the Church to be the friend of the people.

The great questions of the future according to Gibbons were not war, commerce or finance but 'the social question which deals with the amelioration of the condition of the great masses of people and especially the working class'. It was a matter of justice for the Church to take their side. With Manning, whom he quoted, he thought that 'The condition of the lower classes which one finds at present amongst our people cannot and must not continue. On such a base no social edifice can be sustained.'

When he moved to the Knights, the Cardinal was even more forthright. He said that to condemn them would be both ridiculous and foolhardy. He reminded Rome that its condemnation of a single priest, whom he did not name, but clearly McGlynn was the priest in question, had done great harm because he was regarded as the friend of the people. What would then occur were Rome to strike at the people themselves in the exercise of their legitimate rights as members of the Knights? He reminded the Romans that about half their 500,000 membership was Catholic and stated bluntly, and probably effectively, that any condemnation of the Knights would lessen the prestige of the Holy See and cut savagely into American funding of the Vatican.

A few days later, Gibbons wrote again to Simeoni.[14] He believed it was neither useful nor opportune to condemn the works of George who, in any case, had only plagiarised the works of Herbert Spencer and John Stuart Mill. As proof, Gibbons referred to an article in the November 1886 *Contemporary Review* and he remarked that the world would regard it as rather singular to attack the works of a humble American writer and not his masters. At the very least, if Rome wanted to do that it would be wise to ask opinions of both Manning and Newman first.

In the judgement of Gibbons, George was neither a socialist nor a communist and did not attack the right to private property, but only wanted an extension of State power over land. Furthermore, the question was so complex that it would be unintelligible to most Americans who, being neither ideologues nor visionaries, were not interested in speculative theories. Finally, it would be unwise to give George's works undue publicity as, being impractical, they would soon run their course. Gibbons then sent his two letters to Manning in London who wrote back to say that he agreed fully and that he had read nothing in George which he felt ought to be condemned.[15]

Despite the misgivings and good sense of Gibbons, Leo was outraged at the clear recalcitrance of McGlynn and, in any case, action was already underway. Under the aegis of Propaganda Fide, it was decided to embark on a thorough investigation of McGlynn which necessarily entailed considerable reference to the teachings of George. A Commission of three cardinals, Virga, Zigliara and Mazzella had started work, and Mazzella was entrusted with the task of summing up the case against McGlynn and George at the end of the investigation. Camillo Mazzella was a Jesuit who had been recently elevated to the College of Cordinals. He had some claim to knowledge of the intellectual and social climate in the United States as he had spent several years in exile there during the Risorgimento and the political process of Italian unification. He had taught theology and was Dean of the Jesuit College at Woodstock before returning to teach at the Jesuit-run Gregorian University in Rome. Mazzella was not disposed to treat the matter of McGlynn lightly because he was a man of decidedly centralist and conservative views, as well as of considerable learning.

Mazzella began his case by recognising that, while the social question was a most difficult and complicated matter, it was also the main problem of the day. Some wanted to solve it by declaring private ownership of land against the natural law, while others, with greater modesty, wanted to achieve the abolition of private property 'by a progressive tax on landed property'. Mazzella put McGlynn amongst the moderate group, but derided the priest as one who held that, rather than Leo, George was the 'Redeemer of the poor' and his personal 'Holy Father'. The recommendations put to Leo were twofold.

Firstly, the Pope should get McGlynn to come to Rome forthwith and, in the event that he did not appear, should excommunicate him. Secondly, it was necessary to examine

George's 'teachings' and, without condemning the author, take the opportunity to issue a pontifical document in which 'the censurable teachings contained [in George's] writings are scrutinised, as well as others like them'. All in all, Mazzella thought that it was time for a profound and mature examination of the whole social question.[16]

In the event, on 6 February 1889, Henry George joined those others through the centuries whose works had been placed on the Index of Forbidden Books. Probably in response to the warnings that reaction to the step in America might be worse than the alleged disease, it was decided to refrain from making public the fact that the books were on the Index.

McGlynn again refused to comply with the demand that he appear in Rome, and sent a telegram to Simeoni which was explicit in his rejection of Roman authority. In case it was not received, he asked the secretary of the United Labor Party of the State of New York, on whose executive committee he now served as chairman and treasurer, to write to Simeoni under the Party letterhead with a copy of the telegram. Gaybert Barnes, secretary of the Party, apparently had excellent Latin or perhaps McGlynn undertook the translation for him. He included McGlynn's telegram, also in Latin with this letter. 'I shall never retract the doctrines I have taught; I shall not come to Rome; I will make no recourse nor have anything to do with your tribunal before which I have no case to answer. I revoke and repudiate everything that any of my officious friends may have tried to do for me in this matter.'[17]

On 3 July 1888, McGlynn was duly excommunicated despite the earlier plea on his behalf by Mary Lanier of Birmingham, Alabama, who wrote to Leo himself on 6 January, 1888.[18] She said that 'there lives no purer, truer priest' than Dr McGlynn 'who is an earnest seeker of the poor, the sick, the dying, the help of the sinner, the friend of the friendless', but who has finally been 'crushed by envy'. She begged Leo to write to him and call him back to the Church, but either Corrigan or Leo was adamant. McGlynn made his peace with the Church in later years.

Despite the caution with which the George affair was handled, his activities remained a source of concern in the Vatican and there was some public knowledge of the decision taken on his books. Those who saw in George only the figure of a persuasive zealot were partially mistaken and Manning, with his judgement that George was a moderate, sensible man, was much closer to the mark. It is certain that George had a deep and lasting effect on his hearers and readers, especially among the poorer classes.

William Lane, in his own way an Australian prophet and dreamer, summed up George's influence well. 'Karl Marx struck deeper than George, and earlier, but Marx only wrote for the schoolmen and the enthusiasts through whom his theories are slowly filtering down, while George wrote in the language of the people for the people and with a force and fire that only one of the people could feel . . .' William Morris Hughes, later prime minister of Australia, reflected on the impact of George's visit to Australia in 1890. He saw something in George that was probably apparent to the three Roman cardinals who examined his writings. Hughes wrote, 'Henry George, with his panacea for all economic and social ills — the single tax — captured the imagination of thousands of young and ardent spirits. Single Tax Leagues sprang up as if by magic and converts, fired by enthusiasm, went about like the early Christians preaching their gospel. And multitudes heard them and enlisted under their banner.' Finally, another Australian, Frank Cotton, put into context the promise of the Californian messiah. In his view, were George's theories adopted 'we might sweep onward and upward to reach at last the Kingdom of God upon earth, which the greatest of all democrats, the purest of all socialists, Jesus of Nazareth, taught his disciples to work, to pray, and if need be, to die for, the Reign of the Prince of Peace.'[19]

Whatever the intrinsic merit of George's theories, if indeed they had any merit at all, it is certain that conservative reactions to George were widespread and not the least in the

Vatican itself. It is scarcely conceivable that a doctrine which bade fair to strike at the source of wealth vested in landed property would awaken no other response than enthusiasm in some of those who heard or read him. Again, it was from the Antipodes that a comment came, and this time directly to Leo himself. Thomas Waddell held 'an important public position' in Sydney and he became alarmed that George was moving about Australia 'advocating his pernicious theory which if put into practice would ruin thousands who have devoted the hard earnings of a lifetime to buy a piece of land to make a home on.' Though Waddell claimed to have read *Progress and Poverty*, he clearly had not understood George who never advocated that land used for dwellings be interfered with.

Although not a Catholic, Waddell wanted Leo's opinion on the book and, especially, that section of it where George 'advocates that the freehold land of every man be taken from him *without compensation* and given back to the state which he says should be the only landlord'. Somehow, Waddell was aware that the Vatican had taken notice of George because he had heard that 'some years ago your attention was drawn to this matter and that you condemned Mr George's proposal as most unfair'. It was almost as if Waddell thought that cricket, or some such English game, was a favourite pastime in the Vatican whereby George's tactics would be quickly seen as 'unfair'. In any case, Waddell wanted to know whether Leo 'as a distinguished Christian gentleman holding the exalted position which you do' had indeed arrived at a negative opinion on George and, if such were the case, it was important that he make it known publicly because Leo's word would carry 'immense weight'. There is no evidence that Waddell received an answer from Leo or from Propaganda.[20]

From the English-speaking world one other, short letter arrived in Rome which touched directly on the social question, but again, it was not from a bishop or priest. Joseph Slavin wrote directly to Propaganda Fide to demand that something be done about the introduction of an eight-hour day which, Slavin alleged, was an old Catholic, Saxon custom. He thought that overwork was destroying faith because people were now used 'like cattle' and they lived in a slavery worse than that which existed before the introduction of steam. It was imperative that the hours of work for women and children be shortened and he also wanted the old Chartist planks of triennial parliaments and payment of members introduced, as well as republican forms of government on the grounds that it was everywhere apparent how kings had let the papacy down. Finally, he warned that 'under the pretext of justice, in other words the rights of men, Socialists are doing their best to destroy Christianity'. Whoever received this letter at Propaganda Fide pencilled on it 'Lo Scrivente è un pazzo'. (The writer is a madman.), and, presumably, went away satisfied.[21]

By early July 1890, Leo had decided, or been persuaded, that some action in relation to the social question was necessary. Unlike his predecessors, he had already proved that he was convinced of the usefulness of addressing letters to the bishops and a steady stream of encyclicals had flowed from his pen over the first decade of his reign. He set out his design in the first encyclical, *Inscrutabili*, dated 21 April 1878, which was directed mainly at the effects on Italy of the movement towards unification and its dire results for the Church. At the beginning of the encyclical he wrote that he 'felt moved by an urgent desire and, as it were by necessity, to address you by letter . . . to strengthen you who are called to share our solicitude, that you may help us to carry on the battle now being waged on behalf of the Church of God and the salvation of souls'.[22]

It is understandable that Leo was so prompt to take up the encyclical as his main measure to promulgate Catholic teaching to the world. The last, far-reaching, formulation of Catholic teaching had taken place at the Council of Trent in the sixteenth century in response to the new doctrines of the Reformation. Although the First Vatican Council of 1870 had been looked forward to with hope, it was not possible for any further developments on the level of dogma, given the proroguing of the

Council in July and the subsequent occupation of Papal Rome by Italian troops on 20 September. After 1870, Pio Nono was a lone and somewhat pathetic figure as, in his declining years, he successfully upheld the dignity of his office while Victor Emmanuel ruled Italy from the erstwhile papal palace on the Quirinal. The simple equation of political power with international prestige and influence was enough to cause the papacy to be held in widespread contempt by those who thought they were witnessing the last days of that ancient Petrine office which went back long before Charlemagne and even Constantine himself.

When Leo turned to the pen with a series of encyclical letters, he was received, initially with some surprise, but, gradually, and especially among Catholics, he was listened to with considerable interest and attention. While his encyclicals did not have as their objective the definition of Catholic faith, they nevertheless performed the important function of applying the teaching of the Church to the contemporary problems of social and political life. To that end, Leo wrote on such matters as Christian Philosophy, Liberty, Marriage, Freemasonry, Civil Government, the Christian Constitution of States, on Socialism and on Slavery. His teaching was firmly rooted in the philosophy of Aquinas, but it was distilled through his own mind and experience.

By the late 1880s, it was taken for granted in the Catholic episcopate that Leo would eventually turn his attention to the social question. In America, where the press and the printed word generally, were fundamental means of communication, some of the bishops thought that the problem of George and, to a lesser extent that of the now excommunicated McGlynn, should be dealt with by means of an encyclical. By 1888, several of them were calling for an encyclical, notably Elder of Cincinnati who wrote to their representative in Rome, Dennis O'Connell specifying that the document should concern itself with the whole social question and not simply the theories propounded by George. Gibbons also wrote again and continued to express his uneasiness about any condemnation of George.[23]

Clearly the idea was acceptable in some quarters in Rome that Leo should again take up the pen, but O'Connell wrote to Archbishop Ireland on 23 July 1888 saying that 'at the Vatican and elsewhere, it is clearly felt that the Pope's policy miscarried and that after his death a new policy must be pursued. They felt that princes in whom they trusted have failed them and that in the future they must turn to the people. The force of events is teaching them truths they would not have listened to from anyone else.'[24] Leo's critics in the Vatican were as mistaken about the Pope's ability to survive, despite his age, as they were about his determination to listen to, and learn from, his times.

Four

The Task Begins

The stage was now set for an encyclical. The problem remained that Leo himself had only theoretical and general notions on the social question, the practical echoes of which had reached him from afar. Furthermore, there did not seem to be anyone near him in the Vatican with the necessary expertise and it was unlikely that he would turn elsewhere for assistance, as it was generally accepted that, in such matters, Leo was his own man. Once the decision to write was taken, all that remained was to find a suitable author of a working draft for an acceptable encyclical on a matter which Leo had become convinced was of unique importance. In the event, what was to become *Rerum Novarum* was not easy either in its inception or in its completion.

Nevertheless, work on the encyclical was underway by early 1890, but it was not begun in the papal quarters within the Vatican. That is not to say that Leo remained aloof from its composition, or that it bore no trace of his thinking. Indeed, from first to last, the Pope followed its composition, sentence by sentence. He made its authors begin again and again until he was satisfied. As a proud and skilful Latinist, Leo watched, hawklike, over the Latin translation until, finally, the text was complete and polished, ready to be given to the worldwide episcopate from the Vatican. The men who wrote it remained silent and everyone accepted it as Leo's. In large measure, they were right to do so.

Domenico Tardini, later cardinal, was an Under-Secretary of State in the Vatican during the years of the Second World War. Time dragged heavily on his hands as many of the normal channels of diplomatic activity to the Vatican were cut off and, perhaps, he wanted to escape mentally from the horrors into which Europe was being plunged. The approach of the fiftieth anniversary of Rerum Novarum, 15 May 1941, caused him to wonder how the original work was done and by whom. He was in a unique position to find out because, unlike other scholars to whom the Archivio Segreto Vaticano was closed for Leo's pontificate, Tardini was able to go directly to the sources. He already knew that, in the Archives of Extraordinary Ecclesiastical Affairs, there were many autographical manuscripts of previous popes. Leo, however, was not among them. After a diligent search, he came across a large body of material in the Archives of the Secretariat of the State. It was made up of letters and telegrams from many parts of the world dealing with and, most frequently, congratulating Leo on the encyclical. All were dated after its publication, so they threw no light at all on the actual composition of the document.[1]

Eventually, in that section of the Secret Archives called *Epistolae ad Principes*, he discovered the papers of Monsignor Alessandro Volpini whom Leo had appointed Secretary of Latin Letters in 1884. When the Pope so desired, Volpini was the principal Latin translator of the text of Leo's encyclicals and other official Vatican documents. Volpini's papers contained the original drafts, corrections, translations and, finally, some of the page proofs of *Rerum Novarum*.[2]

Tardini had all he needed and he began to work through all the documents with the intention of publishing a book on the composition of the encyclical. By the end of the War, with consequent growth in his own duties, Tardini realised that he could never bring his work on the encyclical to fruition. He passed all he had done to a younger scholar, Monsignor Giovanni Antonazzi, who published a splendid volume in 1957 which brought together and commented on all the documents left in the Archives by Volpini.[3] However, it is clear that, without detracting one whit from Antonazzi's work, Tardini had paved the way. His notes, now bound in with Volpini's material in the Secret Archives, attest to that fact.

Tardini set down his most singular discovery succinctly. 'It is a remarkable fact that notwithstanding the most diligent research, *not one single word*, written by that Pope [Leo XIII] for the preparation of *Rerum Novarum* has been found.'[4] Acting on a close examination of other documents, and drawing on oral tradition from the 1890s, which was still alive in Vatican circles in the 1940s, he was able to write, 'It is however known that it was the custom of Leo XIII to indicate personally, but by *word of mouth*, that which ought to be the fundamental direction of papal documents. Under his dictation, those closest to him wrote what he wanted . . . The Pope followed the same method in correcting the proofs. He suggested corrections and others wrote them down.'[5]

Tardini was also aware of Eduardo Soderini's testimony as stated in his study of Leo's pontificate, some of which came to him from Alessandro Volpini with whom Soderini had formed a close friendship. Doubtless based on oral testimony from Volpini, Soderini said that the Pope was not customarily given to composing his own documents, but preferred to direct their construction and they later came out under his own hand.[6] In reference to *Rerum Novarum*, however, Tardini was very cautious. He wrote, 'Perhaps the general lines were given by Leo XIII himself.'[7] The reason for Tardini's prudence on the authorship of the encyclical becomes clear with his comment on the first draft. 'The draft by Father Liberatore is very succinct, but it contains everything that later became the substance of the encyclical.'[8] Without question, Tardini recognised that the primary author of the encyclical was the relatively obscure Jesuit, Matteo Liberatore, whose authorship was established for Tardini on 3 December 1939 by an elderly Vatican prelate, Archbishop Zongli. Zongli was able to recognise and authenticate the symbol used by Liberatore which appears on the first page of the text. Tardini, nonetheless, acknowledged that Leo himself took full and conscious responsibility for the final shape of *Rerum Novarum* which, in that sense, made it his.[9]

It is highly likely that, when Leo finally decided that an encyclical on the social question was necessary, he made it plain to the prospective author that some degree of haste was required. Hence, Liberatore, now in his eightieth year, wasted no time. He composed an Italian text of about six thousand words which proved to be less than a third the length of the final version. It is uncertain when Liberatore began his draft, but it was probably about April 1890 as it was passed to Volpini for translation into Latin on 5 July, 1890.[10] An examination of Liberatore's Italian text makes another thing abundantly clear. The Jesuit knew that he was writing a draft which would be worked over and probably reworked again. As a consequence, he concentrated on the sense without much consideration for style, punctuation or precision in references to Biblical texts.[11]

'La Questione Operaia' (The Worker Question) was the simple, Italian title which Liberatore gave to his text but, in so doing, he set the whole tone of the document. He also thereby indicated that, in Leo's mind, it was the worker question that the encyclical had to address and very probably, it was under that title, that it was discussed in the papal quarters when Liberatore was given his commission. Certainly, the encyclical had to range over many issues, but it all came back to the problem of the workers themselves. When Volpini put Liberatore's title into Latin it read as 'De Conditione Opificum' because, in essence, Liberatore had addressed himself to the condition of the workers so that the title stood there to bring home immediately to its readers that the workers were the meat and purpose of the encyclical.[12]

Mindful, perhaps, of those same workers, Liberatore did not use the royal plural normally associated with papal documents and, in the very first paragraph, he strove to associate Leo with the poor and to express the concern of the Pope for them. He began:

Vicar of that very God who wants to be present in the poor, 'I was hungry and you gave me to eat, naked and you covered me', I am unable to prevent myself being overcome by a hallowed and profound sense of compassion at the sight of the poor. At this moment, anyone who refuses to allow himself to be deceived must admit that the condition in which the greater part of the working class finds itself is indeed miserable.[13]

Liberatore went on to deplore the riots and tumults which seemed to threaten the social order but he was quick to see their causes. Hunger lay at their root and a father, whose heart was stricken at the cries of his children for whom he was unable to provide bread, often had nowhere to turn. In times of commercial crisis, he often found himself without work. Even in normal times, the meagre wage he was paid only permitted a 'miserable and squalid existence', notwithstanding his own constant labours and those moreover of his wife and children.[14]

In the opinion of the Jesuit, this state of affairs had its origins in the Revolution of the past century which, by suppressing the old corporations of the workers without replacing them with anything, broke the bonds between workers and owners. The workers, now isolated and defenceless, were thus thrown into the arms 'of an individualism without heart which is constrained neither by safeguards nor law'. Capitalism then proceeded to reproduce in another form, that practice of usury already condemned by the Church and 'subjected society to the tyranny of money'. From that flowed 'the boundless wealth of some who thus became all powerful with the consequent impoverishment of the rest'. Composed as it was of the weak, the disorganised and the dispersed, the working class was the principal sufferer and 'This class has an absolute need of being lifted up again'.[15]

In this introduction, the shades are evident of Vogelsang and those who looked back to a glorious past which the Revolution had shattered and capitalism had further destroyed. The socialists in particular, and, perhaps, even Henry George, follow when the concept of public ownership is excoriated. To the Jesuit ' the so-called nationalisation of land and capital is an iniquitous usurpation, forbidden by law whether natural, positive or divine'. Liberatore upheld the absolute and inalienable right to the possession of private property, whether in land or in goods, while admitting that the State could modify and regulate that right for the common good, but never abolish it. To abolish it would certainly produce a form of equality, but it would be 'equality in debasement, in sloth and in destitution' because it would dry up the very wells of riches by stamping out individual inventiveness and industry.[16]

In his next section, Liberatore confronted the problem of population control which, hitherto, had no resonance whatever in papal documents and only in a rudimentary form in moral theology. He based his analysis on Malthusian concepts of the need to restrict population growth because of the alleged lack of future resources of the earth. In a forthright manner, he rejected the validity of the thesis in itself and, more particularly, the means proposed to remedy the problem either through State intervention to restrict marriages or through birth control. The first was a violation of a fundamental human right while the second was even worse. It was 'an execrable violation of the order of nature' which God Himself had punished with instant death in the person of Onan. Switching to the royal plural, Liberatore had Leo saying, 'We exhort the zeal of Bishops and Priests so that with all their strength they may oppose themselves to such a nefarious custom which, by the work of wicked men, is getting a foothold in and is being diffused in Christian countries.'[17] It was a rash but prescient step of Liberatore to want to include this section in the encyclical, even if his rejection of Malthusianism is at odds with some scientific and much popular opinion in a later period.

Certainly aware of the arguments that had so agitated the participants at Liège, Liberatore, nonetheless, had no hesitation in coming down on the side of the interventionists in respect of the role of the State in the worker question. The State had no other purpose than to produce the good of its citizens and, in any given State, the workers formed the majority of the citizens, which meant that their needs were unquestionably a responsibility of the State. Furthermore, as the first citizens the State had to concern itself with were the weak, the workers were of primary consideration because they, without political power and wealth, were themselves numbered among the weak. As a result, the State had a primary duty to interest itself in the welfare of worker associations which should never be proscribed, but rather be given complete freedom, as well as the right to acquire property. The State had to refrain from any interference in the internal affairs of worker associations because to do so would easily lead to their being stifled by outside control.[18]

While it was one thing to assert the rights of worker associations to freedom and protection, it was another to insist upon the role of the State in the actual field of wages and conditions. Liberatore was no less forthright that the State had the duty to intervene because public morality and justice both demanded that such matters could never 'be abandoned to the use of individual freedoms and the right to enter into contracts' which simply reiterated the point made by Manning for years in London.[19] The conditions under which children and women worked, the health of adults and days of rest were matters which the Revolution, following the old and vicious ideas of liberalism, had left to the strong to control, thus giving freedom where its use was most repugnant and denying it to the weak who needed it most.

The Jesuit went into some detail on regulating the hours of work for women, children and miners. He said that the bread winner ought never to be driven to exhaustion by excessive work, but ought to be enabled to obtain a living by moderate labour for himself and those dependent upon him.[20] In his insistence on the observance of Sundays and feast days, both because of the sanctity of religion and the need for rest, Liberatore said that Saturday work hours should be diminished or, better still, halved, to ensure that the worker might achieve a truly fruitful period of repose.[21]

The initiative taken by William II to call a Conference in Berlin for March 1890, to reach an international agreement to assist the working class, had clearly impressed Liberatore. He wrote two brief articles on it for *Civiltà Cattolica* which appeared in mid-February and early March before he began work on the encyclical, which indicates that he began his draft at a later date.[22] In every country, the child, the woman and the worker were much the same, with the same needs and rights. An international agreement of some kind was clearly necessary, because unilateral regulation of working conditions could put in jeopardy the country which enacted the legislation or those that omitted to do so.

Liberatore congratulated the Kaiser on the results of the Conference and looked to individual governments which would put its deliberations into effect. He hoped, moreover, that other conferences would follow which would learn from the experience of the first and profit by the development of other ideas.[23] Leo had taken note already of the fact that William had recognised the need for 'the free activity of the Church, in order that the laws by which work was regulated would become fruitful' and wrote to him with warm congratulations, but had refrained from sending a special representative from the Holy See, despite the invitation to do so. He felt that it was sufficient that the Bishop of Breslau be present at the Conference.[24]

With that as his premise, the Jesuit launched into the problem that he clearly saw as central to a great deal of the worker question and which, in his estimation, 'reduced the whole working class to slavery'. Monopolies, coalitions of large capital, playing the money market, risky and fraudulent speculation all tended to ruin small industry, produce unemployment and cause harmful rises in the cost of living. In those circumstances, governments had to intervene, even if by so doing they upset the liberals who, with their doctrine of laissez-faire, had already brought great harm to the economic and political sectors of communities in capitalist societies. From this same source, a 'bloody plague' of modern industry in the form of strikes had arisen. Essentially, the workers struck because they had at their disposal no other means with which to fight for their rights. To confront that problem, Liberatore suggested that mixed committees of owners and workers be set up with some degree of legal acceptance. It would be their task, jointly and authoritatively, to decide disputes over wages and conditions.[25]

It is scarcely surprising that Liberatore should see the solution for a good many of the ills besetting the workers as lying within their own grasp. He had lived his life in an Italy only marginally touched by the Industrial Revolution, which was especially the case in Rome and in the south of Italy. He had only theoretical concepts of worker organisations and, in particular, of the trade union movement. Given the manifest rejection by that movement in continental Europe of any connection between religion and social progress, it was unlikely that he would look to it as the organisational shape of the working class. Yet, he, at no time, wished to see the workers either exhorted to resign themselves to their miserable fate or to rely on the benevolence and patronage of the rich and powerful, whom he had already excoriated for their contempt for the workers. Nonetheless, in a document so full of a profound awareness of the pressing need for a solution, it is almost startling to find Liberatore proposing corporations as the means of renewal, as the expression of united strength among the workers, and as the remedy for class warfare. He began the fifth section of his draft with, 'The remedy for the evils which beset the working class must come from the workers themselves. And in what way? Through the Corporation.'[26]

Even were it the case that the medieval guilds had a profound and beneficial effect on society and, in particular, on the workers themselves, the important fact was that no organised forms of the workforce existed at that distant time. As a result, no model from the pre-industrial era could be adapted in any adequate manner for the late nineteenth century. Admittedly, the example of Karmel in France seemed to hold out hope for the revival of the old system. What was forgotten, or overlooked, was that

Karmel's experiment was a result of the initiative of an owner and that worker representation in respect of wages and conditions was minimal. The other factor which had made an impression on Liberatore and moved him to state his preference for corporations was the long-standing conviction of the Italian *Opera dei Congressi* that only through corporations, or some similar form of mixed unions, would industrial peace be achieved. One of the leaders of the *Opera*, Andrea Cappellazzi, said in 1890, 'The real and reasonable vindication of the worker is in the re-establishment of the corporations of the Middle Ages and not in strikes.'[27]

Certainly, Liberatore was careful to reject any form of State intervention in the actual setting up of the corporations, nor did he engage in any fanciful concepts by seeing them as the basis of a new State. Their role was to be essentially mediatory, given their mixed membership. Their main, practical function was to act as welfare bodies, as societies of mutual aid which would give practical help to the workers in their time of need when industry was unable, temporarily, to find work for them. In sickness, old age and during an unforeseen crisis or after an accident, the corporation would come to the aid of the workers. On the moral level, apart from dampening the fires of industrial conflict, Liberatore saw the corporations as having their primary role in the restoration of domestic relations. What effect the old guilds had on family life was never clear, but the new corporations were expected to 'restore the children to parental education, the mother to domestic cares and of the father to the headship of the family'.[28]

Unquestionably, the section on corporations in Liberatore's draft was the weakest and he seemed to have been unaware that they had been rejected as a solution by the majority of the Catholic theorists in Europe, while, to the English and the Americans, they were never in practical contention. Apart from their basis in the medieval world, the text never made it plain how the corporations were to be set up, or by whom. As if he were unsure himself of the strength of his case, he even mixed up his terminology by speaking of Congregations with a religious and moral purpose, and Christian Corporations which seemed to share the same purpose.[29]

In his enthusiasm for an overall solution to the Social Question as it affected the workers, worse confusion was to follow. Liberatore's purpose was to arrive at the need for a just wage, which eventually became the cardinal point of his argument. But he began badly by a lengthy section in which he said that, if the corporations were to fulfil their purpose, they would need a ready supply of funds which the workers, on the basis of their savings, could scarcely provide and hence the need for the rich to step in and be generous. This led to a tortured argument which started with the proposition that 'God wanted the human race to be divided into two ranks, the rich and the poor' so that they may complement each other.[30] Basing his case on quotes from Scripture and Aquinas, he then worked his way through the obligation of the rich to share their superabundance with the poor, and concluded by stating that helping to set up stable bodies such as corporations was a far more fruitful way of assisting those among the poor who were most deserving, i.e. the workers, than giving alms.[31]

Liberatore then came to the vexed question of wages. In his opinion, economic science needed profound reorientation in this matter, even though it had to retain its three fundamentals in capital, profit and wages. The first two were based on the unshakeable principle of property, while the concept of a wage stemmed from the impossibility of everyone becoming a capitalist and, hence, the wage system was there to stay. On the basis of such tenuous propositions, Liberatore, nonetheless, proceeded to a developed and penetrating analysis of wages.

> *Whatever else, a wage is not a price, because work is not mere merchandise. To work is to engage in a human act and, therefore, it is an extension of the human personality. A wage which arises from work is not determined by nature. It is necessary that it be arrived at by an act of the human will*

and therefore in virtue of a contract. But such a contract cannot be regulated by the same law of supply and demand which is appropriate in the case of merchandise. It must be governed by the laws of justice and equity, commensurate to the purpose for which work was imposed by God on man. That purpose is the sustenance of the worker as he is understood by nature and, therefore, not only as an individual person, but even more as husband and father. In other words the wage is intended for the sustenance of the worker and his family. Up to this point it is a question of justice and below that it is not licit to descend. 'In the sweat of your brow you will earn your bread.[32]

If the strict payment of a family wage arose from the demands of pure justice, equity suggested, and charity demanded, something more, in order that the worker, as well as merely providing for himself and his family, should enjoy some degree of well-being and, indeed, be in a position to better his own lot in life and that of this family. Liberatore went so far as to work out a kind of simple formula to express his thought. The owner put in his capital, the means of production and his own expertise in running the operation and, consequently, he was entitled to a just profit. Once that was assured, the rest ought to be spent in raising wages.

While equity suggested such a way of acting, Liberatore had the feeling that such a state of affairs might encounter some difficulty in realisation in the world at large, so he said that charity had to be the yardstick. Such charity was likely to be found only in the corporations in which all would make up one family of workers and owners in Christ. They would be known as such exactly because they proved by their love for each other that they were His followers.[33]

The worker, whom Liberatore considered the most deserving of just, equitable and charitable consideration, was the farm labourer who, although his work was the most necessary for the sustenance of the human race, was often so badly paid that he starved and did not even 'taste the fruits of that earth he watered with his sweat and made fertile with his hard work'.[34] Clearly, he was familiar with the gradual depopulation of the countryside in Italy, the clustering of the farm labourers in villages from which they often had to walk long journeys to work on land in which they had lost their personal involvement, the diseases that so frequently prevailed through poor nourishment and the widespread demoralisation of large segments of the rural community. Again, the corporations, and especially those in Germany in which the workers became part proprietors, were looked to as a remedy for this state of affairs and held up as an example for the emulation of others.[35]

Liberatore then went on to give an explanation of the role of the Church in the worker question through preaching, educating and engaging in works of charity. With a gentle reproof to those whose misery stemmed not so much from low or fluctuating wages as from a disordered way of life, Liberatore had Leo taking a resolute stand on behalf of the bishops and priests, religious and laity who involved themselves on the side of the workers. Whether they did it by protecting worker organisations, helping them with assistance, mediating between the workers and the owners, promoting the study of the whole complex question of relations between the classes in a search for solutions or, finally, by setting up religious institutes on behalf of the working class, all such activities were a source of great joy to the Pope and the Jesuit had him expressing the hope that they would flourish and succeed.[36]

Finally, the necessary prerequisite for the Church, were it to be of maximum benefit to humanity, was that it enjoy the freedom to exercise its salvific ministry. Liberatore reminded those European governments who seemed bent on nullifying any positive action on the part of the Church that they thereby 'deprived themselves of the most useful help they could receive from the free activity of the Church' and Liberatore had Leo recalling to his readers that he had pleaded for such freedom for the Church in the past.[37] Nevertheless, if States were so foolish as to invite their own destruction by that kind of behaviour, it remained the duty of all the clergy to use whatever freedom they still possessed for the greater good of the people and, especially, for the working class who needed them the most.

With all its faults of imprecision, wishful thinking and paternalism, the draft written by Liberatore was a noble document, in particular, those sections of it which dealt with the evils of capitalism and the demand for a family wage. For the first time since the Industrial Revolution, the Church and the Papacy were firmly lined up on the side of the workers. The draft did not deny the fact of industrial strife between employers and employees. It admitted that there were serious grounds for conflict, deplored the violence that sometimes ensued and laid the blame squarely on those who crushed the workers. That its main solution was seen to lie in the utopian concept of corporations said much more than that the Church was merely looking back to a long-gone era. It was an acknowledgement that the solution to the problem of the workers was perhaps beyond resolve, at least with those means Liberatore was prepared to recognise. Without the further step of a decisive recognition in an unequivocal manner of the existence, the rights and the power of the trade union movement, the solutions proposed had perforce to remain fanciful. As for Liberatore, old and infirm, but still a scholar of wide knowledge and compassion, he had made an initial contribution to *Rerum Novarum*. Nonetheless, the work had just begun.

Five

Liberatore Revised

Liberatore's draft never achieved permanency, even in a Latin translation. It was not intended to be other than a rough, working document which would serve as a starting point from which a more refined and elaborate final draft would follow. After Leo, and probably others, had read it, the draft was passed to the Dominican scholar, Cardinal Zigliara, in September 1890. It was his task to polish Liberatore's Italian draft and make it ready for translation into Latin.

Zigliara was a leading Thomist who, since 1880, had been working with two other scholars on the Leonine edition of the writings of Thomas Aquinas. He was Corsican-born but, during Archbishop Pecci's days in Perugia, he had worked closely with him, and, as a result, he was created cardinal in Leo's first consistory in 1879. Zigliara was deeply imbued with scholastic and Thomistic thought, but he had not worked as seriously on the social question as Liberatore who had both taught and written on it. As a consequence, he could only bring a few new points to the draft. What he had to offer was an ordered and structured mind. He could also make sure that the final version was ideologically sound. Since it is certain that a degree of unease had been expressed about some of the Jesuit's propositions, it would be expected that a more formal and less outspoken reworking would ensue. Whatever else, it is clear that economy of thought, so evident in Liberatore, was no part of Zigliara's makeup. His version was over twice as long as the Jesuit's sparse and succinct document.[1]

Zigliara's draft retained the title, 'The Worker Question' but he saw it as both 'difficult' and 'threatening', which diminished the positive light in which Liberatore had placed it. His first few lines set the tone. The idea of a pope who saw himself as Vicar of God made flesh in the poor was discarded. Zigliara's pope was a Roman Pontiff called by providence to rule a Church which had the task of telling the world unfailingly that, being the way, the truth and the life of mankind, its duty was 'to warn against dangers, help the needy, bring the errant back to the truth and maintain individuals, peoples and Governments in the way of justice and honesty'. Therefore, just as Liberatore's introduction stemmed from Christ's words of identification with the poor, Zigliara's stood upon the statement of the same Christ who was to him the awesome Pantocrator, 'I am the way, the truth and the life.'[2] In such a scheme of things, there was little room left to manoeuvre because rigid parameters had been set in which the Church was central. Liberatore had made Christ, the poor and, especially, that section of the poor called the workers, central to his whole draft.

Although the major directions traced out by Liberatore were followed in Zigliara, indeed he frequently used the exact words of the former, there were nonetheless some additions and omissions. The right to private property was dealt with at even greater length, with a more direct and definitive rejection of socialism. Its theories, rather than solving the worker question, were held to aggravate it, to the disadvantage of the workers themselves, and result in a great injustice because socialism is injurious 'to the rights inherent in the nature of man and is contrary to the duties of the State'. Unnamed as in Liberatore, both McGlynn and Henry George were given fuller treatment and their opinions, summed up as 'the discordant voices of a few utopians', were rejected out of hand as contrary to common sense, the natural law and, finally, the divine law itself.[3]

More cautious than Liberatore, who asserted without equivocation the right in justice to a family wage, Zigliara nonetheless spoke of the needs of the family in a context that seemed to assume some such right. He agreed with Liberatore that it was against justice for the owner or capitalist to pay a wage inadequate to the needs of 'the worker himself'.[4] Capitalist was a word not used by Liberatore, but Zigliara spoke of 'voracious capitalists who, in their lust for inordinate gain, demand from the worker toil of such a kind that he is morally broken and his physical strength is exhausted to the extent that he dies prematurely'.[5]

Nonetheless, Zigliara held that the rich had the right to retain enough of their profits to satisfy the needs and reasonable requirements of their own position and that of their families, before being obliged in charity to do anything for the poor. Zigliara could not bring himself to apply that same form of reasoning in reverse for the poor who, having little or nothing were frequently unable to satisfy the basic needs of themselves and their families. Indeed, poverty itself was defined as consisting principally in 'the desire to have more than one already has', and for Christians, fortified with the riches of the spirit which broke or entirely removed all inordinate desire for earthly wealth, material poverty was scarcely of any consequence. Such a line of reasoning was based on the principle that the Church in the normal course of events always began by attending to the needs of the soul because 'poverty and misery of the body are as nothing compared to the miseries of the spirit'.[6]

It would be unfair to Zigliara not to stress that he laid great emphasis on the charitable works of the Church and the need for their continuation, as well as the right of the Church to be free from interference by the State in the exercise of such works. He also wrote at some length on the quality and quantity of work, comparing the arduous forms of work done in mines or in stiflingly hot factories with that done in the open air; the need to make provisions for the elderly and the young and, especially, for women, whom he saw as 'formed by nature for domestic work'; the demand for full employment with the requirement that 'the worker never lacks employment', and the protection that must be afforded the worker against unjust contracts.[7]

Nevertheless, much more than Liberatore, Zigliara stressed the tendency of many workers to dissipate their wages in vice and in forms of insobriety and he praised the truly Christian worker in words which, although well-intended, scarcely helped solve the very real problems encountered everywhere in the industrialised world, which he himself recognised as pressing on the workers. Indeed, to Zigliara, the Christian worker should live alongside the rich without envy, reasonably persuaded that both riches and poverty were works of God. Such a thought, would make him live a life of resignation because he trusts in 'Divine Providence from whose goodness he awaits the daily bread for himself and his family with security, because it has been divinely promised. In fact, such a worker would go even further and find a way to divide that bread with those who are poorer than himself.' He drew upon the ancient tradition of St Leo the Great to uphold his argument when St Leo said that the poor man who is a Christian always has more than he lacks and does not fear to suffer want because God sees to it that he possesses all.[8]

In his treatment of the worker question, it is apparent that Liberatore had set a tone from which Zigliara could not venture to depart and, at times, his language is even more forceful than that of the Jesuit. At the same time, he found it necessary to weave throughout his text a moral and spiritual theme of Christian resignation, which Liberatore never mentioned. More importantly, he moved away from the Jesuit's proposition on a family wage being paid in justice, although he tried to make it plain that, without a family wage, the worker and his family would never be able to live in dignity.

The most notable departure from Liberatore, and, in itself, a healthy one, was the lessened emphasis placed on the role of the corporations by Zigliara who was, nevertheless, in general agreement with Liberatore on the role of the State, which he treated at much greater length. He never used the word corporations, but preferred to speak of 'associations', 'professional communities' or 'professional societies' which tentatively moved away from the old idea of mixed associations made up of employers and workers. He also recognised that such associations were springing up everywhere, by which he meant trade unions, although he never gave them that name. What concerned him most was that such associations were frequently enforced on the workers who were unable to find employment in their trade unless they were members and, furthermore, that the associations were also frequently 'organised and directed by a hand which more or less remains in secret' and in that guise operated in an anti-social and anti-Christian sense. This led him to the need for Christian associations and he praised the Catholic Congresses and the Catholic worker associations that had sprung from the concern of many dedicated men for the cause of the working class.[9]

It was still only twenty years since the demise of the Papal States and Leo remained 'The Prisoner in the Vatican'. Zigliara could not resist dealing with the interference by the State in the rights of the Church. The question of extensive Church property and the consequent relationship of Church to State was confined to Europe and some of the Latin American States, and bore little relevance to the position of the Church in the democratic States, but that did not deter Zigliara. With sentiments redolent more of the days of Innocent III and Boniface VIII, he asserted that the civil State was 'by its nature not superior but subject to the laws of God and His Vicar on earth'. He dwelt at length on the abolition and expulsion of religious orders, enforced military service of the clergy and the silencing of the Catholic press. He then upbraided the way the secular press heaped calumnies on the ministry of the Church while the State interfered with the running of seminaries and withdrew assistance from the clergy. All of this led him to remark how madness had overcome the modern State when it was clear that the worker question 'threatened to overturn the whole social order' while the State deprived itself of the valuable means the Church had to offer for its resolution.[10]

Some satisfaction must have been expressed with Zigliara's draft because it went on unaltered to Volpini who began work immediately on a Latin translation. He did not, however, make much progress. After completing less than one sixth of the text, he made a marginal note on it on 28 October 1890 which said that he had stopped work upon orders from above. His exact words were: '*28 ottobre 1890 Sospeso lavoro per ordine superiore.*'[11] The only source from which such an order could legitimately come was Leo himself, who had probably read Zigliara's draft at that stage and come to the conclusion that it was not satisfactory. Perhaps Volpini drew his own difficulty to the attention of the Pope because his translation was suspended exactly at the point at which, having hinted in a less direct manner than Liberatore at the evil of birth control, Zigliara had passed to the role of the father of a family, the needs of the family itself and the pre-eminence of its role over that of the State. Clearly, such considerations led inevitably to a further analysis of the right to own property and, finally, to the concept of a just wage. To Leo, it was obvious that a further reworking of the draft was necessary and the decision to do so was promptly made.

In the three weeks between 28 October 1890, when Volpini stopped work, and 19 November when he again started on a translation, another draft was written. Those responsible were both Jesuits and it is indicative of Leo's trust in Liberatore that he again called upon him to work on a draft that had started as his own, but had undergone very considerable transformation at the hand of Cardinal Zigliara. The other Jesuit was Cardinal Camillo Mazzella who was familiar with the work of Henry George and had presented the case to Propaganda Fide against Father McGlynn in 1888. It was unlikely that a version under his care would suffer any lessening in an insistence on the right to private property.

The Vatican Archives hold a printed proof of fifty-seven pages and a handwritten manuscript of eighty-eight pages of this third and final Italian draft. There can be little doubt that Liberatore was again its principal author, although the manuscript had not been identified as being in his hand or in that of Mazzella. Yet it contains the same characteristic lack of attention to style, spelling and citation as Liberatore's first draft. Perhaps the elderly Jesuit dictated from notes, using his own original, parts of Zigliara and other amendments he himself wanted to make. As for precision in matters of construction, together with overall uniformity, Liberatore knew he could leave that to the Latinists who would attend to the secondary matters. He did not succeed in eliminating the verbosity of Zigliara by returning to the brevity and precision of his original, but he did put back in large measure, and in his own words, those sections of his draft which he thought needed to be restated. When he translated this third Italian version into Latin, the fact that Volpini noted on the manuscript and on the proof pages that he had worked from Zigliara's draft, 'redone by Card. Mazella and P. Liberatore', means simply that he recognised that the main, transitional point had been Zigliara from Liberatore. Why he ignored the priest's reworking back to his own original may be explained by the reverence shown to the Roman purple, which Liberatore never wore, or to the fact that there was material which Liberatore still wanted included which he or others preferred to eliminate.[12]

Mazzella's contribution to the third draft was minimal, which is not to say that he did not work through it thoroughly and make suggestions and some minor corrections as he saw fit. He had not come to his task with the same degree of involvement or preparation as Liberatore so that he was clearly satisfied to leave the major task to his Jesuit colleague. One decisive comment he did make resulted in the elimination of Liberatore's prescient statement on birth control. Zigliara had already watered down Liberatore's text to a considerable degree by rewriting it to read 'No human law can deprive man of the natural or fundamental right to marriage, or in any way whatever limit the principal scope which God ordained it to have when He said: "Increase and multiply and fill the earth and subdue it." ' (Genesis 1: 28).[13] In the third draft, Liberatore put in the few lines from Zigliara and followed them with all those he had written in the first. He expressed himself in a clearer, more forthright manner to make his, and by extension the Pope's opposition to birth control explicit. Liberatore wrote, 'There is no worse crime than this.' Such a forthright comment was not to Mazzella's satisfaction who wrote in the margin the cryptic question 'Is it expedient to treat of such depravity?' As a consequence, and probably after further consideration by Leo, all Liberatore's words were omitted in the official and final Latin text while those of Zigliara, which said practically nothing, were retained.[14]

The matter of greater importance at the time was the question of what was meant by a just wage. The question had been discussed at much length and with varying degrees of heat at the Catholic Congresses of preceding years without resolution. It was reasonable to expect that a papal pronouncement on the worker question would confront the problem and give a definite ruling. Essentially, the question was simply — was an employer bound in justice to pay a wage which would provide adequate sustenance for a worker and his dependent family, or merely for the sustenance of the worker himself? Liberatore's answer, given in his first draft, was clear. To him, wife and children were united with the worker, not only in a personal, internal bond within the family, but likewise in his work which he performed not merely for himself, but for them also.

Liberatore insisted on this principle for all who laboured and, when speaking of the right to private property, he said that dominion was given both over the fruits of the earth and the earth itself, from which man drew the means to support himself and those for whom he was responsible.[15] Hence, it was part of his total philosophy, based on reasoning flowing from both the divine and natural law, as well as the commonly accepted arrangement of society.

Nonetheless, all that the Jesuit had written on the concept of a family wage was carefully struck from, or modified in the subsequent drafts. Zigliara began the process by abolishing the reference to wife and family when he transformed 'the means to support himself and those who belong to him' into 'the means to serve for his future needs' while 'the sustenance of the worker and his family', became 'the sustenance of the worker himself' and a final reference to earning a living 'for himself and his own with moderate work' was omitted entirely. Even when it came to the Latin version, the translator was very cautious. Where Liberatore's third Italian text spoke of the need for the State to intervene in cases in which the employer did not pay the agreed wage, the marginal note was made that it was necessary to judge whether the wage was proportionate to the work done; the statement that 'it was an act of unjust violence to force a worker to accept conditions that were too hard' was accompanied by the note: 'This must be given further consideration', and when Liberatore said that a wise worker, after taking care of his wife and children, would be able to set enough aside to 'acquire his own small land holding', it was noted: 'Isn't that going too far? It is the Pope who is speaking.'[16]

As the author of the first draft, in which he spelled out the above matters in a much more decisive manner, Liberatore cannot be supposed to have suffered such a remarkable change unaided on questions of very considerable importance. Clearly, only a higher authority in the person of Leo, who was probably prompted by Zigliara, Mazzella, and perhaps others as well, could have persuaded him to amend his text so that a wage was regarded as paid for the sustenance of the worker alone. Distinctions between justice and charity became pointless, as even the most determined idealist realised that, under a burgeoning capitalist system, no employer or owner would conduct his financial arrangements with his employees on the basis of charity. Leo had no intention of putting his name to a document that spoke of a family wage as a matter of justice, while one that saw a relationship between the worker and his family as impinging on the concept of a just wage was too delicate to give full support to, so such references had to be attenuated or elided. That Leo was given credit in history for *Rerum Novarum* and what it contained is justifiable because it covered matters of equally grave importance as the question of a just wage. Nonetheless, such a recognition only enhances further the contribution of Liberatore to what *Rerum Novarum* could have contained.

The remarkable thing is that, somehow, a belief long persisted that Leo in Rerum Novarum had committed himself to the concept of a family wage, even amongst those who surely had every reason to know that such was not the case. In 1952, Marcellino Olaechea Loizaga, Archbishop of Valenza, Spain, wrote a pastoral letter entitled *Salario Justo*, which he followed with another entitled *Alrededor del Salario Justo* in 1953. He held that it was very probable that a family wage had to be paid in commutative justice and he went on in some detail to outline the expenses necessary to keep a family in moderate comfort. Commutative justice meant that, if the owner or employer did not pay a family wage, he was obliged in justice to restore to the worker that portion of the wage that remained unpaid. He admitted, however, that Leo had not solved the problem of restitution in *Rerum Novarum*.[17] The Spanish and European press published excerpts of the Archbishop's pastoral letter and, as a consequence, his ideas achieved widespread notoriety.

In his Introduction, Loizaga used excerpts from *Rerum Novarum* to prove that Leo always spoke of a wage as a family wage. The excerpts were not taken from *Rerum Novarum* itself, but from a work by a Spanish Jesuit, Father Vilacreus, who in his *Orientaciones Sociales* had quoted at length from Leo. But the Jesuit had doctored Leo's text by adding in brackets 'and of that of his family' or an expression that included the family to the six occasions in which the Pope wrote of a wage and the worker. To cite the clearest example. Leo said, 'a wage ought to be sufficient to support a frugal and well-behaved wage earner'. To that Vilacreus had added in brackets 'and his family' without giving the slightest indication that the original contained no such words — with or without brackets.[18] The irony is that Liberatore again came to the fore because, in his original, he always spoke of the worker and his family when he dealt with the question of a wage. He did so without brackets.

In one country, which by many was seen as a living laboratory where the problems of the 'social question' were worked out in practice if not in theory, there was a serious attempt to apply the thoughts of Liberatore as they appeared in the modified version Leo finally accepted as *Rerum Novarum*. In 1907, Henry Bournes Higgins became President of the Australian Commonwealth Court of Conciliation and Arbitration. In his first case, he was faced with the difficult task of deciding whether the manufacturer H.V. McKay was paying a 'fair and reasonable' wage to his employees. Though not a member of the Catholic Church, Higgins had read and commented on *Rerum Novarum* in 1896 and, in deciding the case, he used the concepts it contained and indeed enlarged on them as Liberatore had previously done. He took it that a worker normally was, or would become, a married man with a wife and children and that he had the right to live in 'a condition of frugal comfort estimated by current human standards.'

Using that as his yardstick, Higgins stipulated a wage which, after enquiry, he had decided was 'fair and reasonable'. It is no discredit to Higgins that he failed to acknowledge his debt to *Rerum Novarum* and that he had made its words his own. It is to his great credit that he supplied in his Harvester judgement that element which Liberatore had insisted on, but which *Rerum Novarum* did not include. As a judge, he was able to apply the concept of a just wage which Liberatore had enunciated and his 'basic wage' was 'the rock on which he built his Court'.[19] Nonetheless, even Higgins, and those who followed him, had to recognise that no national wage case could be decided without consideration of the total economy. Then, as always in democratic countries, the distribution of the gross national product was the most important political question faced by governments, unions and arbitration courts.

Six

The Labour of the Latinists

When Leo XIII wanted a job done thoroughly and rapidly, it was not unusual for him to resort to extreme measures. He turned eighty in 1890 but, despite his years, he was capable of sustained work which often resulted in his dictating throughout the entire night. He rarely worked alone and, for the benefit of his exhausted secretary, it was customary for him to call a short break at odd intervals during the night, at which point the secretary would be invited to read aloud an Ode of Horace. Presumably refreshed, they would then return to work. On other occasions Leo would lock his Latin translator in the papal library early in the morning and, at noon, he would appear at the door with a tray on which there was a glass of marsala and a couple of biscuits. By two o'clock work would be over for the day, but there was always the possibility of a night shift if affairs were pressing.

By November 1890, the task of getting *Rerum Novarum* to the printer was urgent and the work fell to two men in particular to bring it to fruition. Alessandro Volpini almost literally spent himself in the service of Leo. In 1903, at the age of fifty-seven, he died a few days before the Pope. Gabriele Boccali was the other Latin translator and he, too, was a close confidant of the Pope. He had been associated with Leo in Perugia and was then called to the Vatican after Leo's election to the papacy. Boccali, like Volpini, was indefatigable in his devotion to Leo and died in 1892, aged forty-nine, within a year of the publication of *Rerum Novarum*. Neither Volpini nor Boccali are remembered by posterity but, in the context of the encyclical, they deserve to be ranked after Liberatore as the principal agents of the final text.

Volpini received Liberatore's and Mazzella's final Italian draft on 17 November 1890. He worked through tirelessly until 31 January 1891, noting that he had completed his Latin translation at five o'clock that afternoon.[1] Perhaps his greatest difficulty with the first draft was rendering thought processes in Latin in a field in which he had not been accustomed to work. Neither Leo, nor his translators, were content to write in medieval Latin. The day had long since passed when papal pronouncements were couched in such a style. Furthermore, men who were accustomed to being invited by their superior to read Horace as a form of relaxation were unlikely to settle for the language of a monastic cellarer of the eleventh century to express the solemn publications of the Vatican during the reign of a Latinist of the calibre of Leo XIII. As a result, Volpini had to think with the mind of an orator of the Roman Republic, while trying to express the thoughts of a social theorist of the nineteenth century. Moreover, he knew that whatever attention Leo paid to the Italian drafts, he was certain to go carefully through the Latin and, if it did not please him, it would all need to be done again.

For a reason which remains unclear, Volpini made no translation of the first forty-nine lines of the Italian draft. However, he stuck with Liberatore's title of 'La Questione Operaia' which he rendered as 'De Conditione Opificum', thus ensuring that the main point of the encyclical was achieved.[2] It was to be dedicated to the condition of the working masses, to the workers themselves and the problems which beset them. Other matters, such as the capitalist system, socialism, unions, corporations, the work of the Church and the involvement of the State were the setting of the workers' problems rather than the main burden of the encyclical itself. To that extent, Leo was staying true to his word of writing an encyclical which would deal with the condition of the workers.

When Volpini got to the section on capitalism, which Liberatore had used to condemn usury in ringing terms and which had survived with some watering down in the final Italian draft, he began to experience difficulties and four agonised, handwritten pages testify to his discomfort. Only by the fourth try, which contains a mere two corrections, was he satisfied.[3] After leaving aside any reference to the Revolution of the past century, he bewailed the loss of the ancient corporations in place of which nothing had been erected, and then he came to capitalism.

He was so determined to make his point that he changed the word capitalism in Liberatore to 'capitalists' and pinned down 'rapacious usury' to the practices of the same 'capitalists'. As a result, the majority of the workers, 'isolated and defenceless' were passed into the hands of hard-hearted employers who operated according to 'the greed of unchecked competition'. He then proceeded to reach new heights in his condemnation of capitalism because he added a sentence which, in ringing tones, spelt out its effects: 'the control of labour and of all kinds of commerce are subject to the will of a few in such a way that a handful of tycoons have been able to put a yoke little better than slavery on the vast masses of the proletariat.'[4]

The next section deals with socialism which, again, Volpini personalised by turning 'Socialismo' into 'Socialistae'. He was not prepared to follow Liberatore in saying that 'the poor are moved by Socialism to hatred and anger at the sight of the rich'. He saw them as merely becoming envious, although he was no less forthright in his denunciation of socialists than Liberatore had been of socialism. Again, those who held to the alleged basic tenet of socialism — the denial of the right to private property — even if they did not belong to any organised body which propogated socialist doctrine, were socialists. This statement was surely intended to give pause for thought to Henry George and Father McGlynn, given their attitude to land ownership.[5]

Indeed, the argument for the right to possess private property, notwithstanding the attitude of 'the upholders of obsolete notions' and opinions held by a few dissidents, is spelled out at great length and in almost tedious detail. Anyone who could assert that men had the right to the use of the fruits of the earth, but not to the land itself, were mere utopianists whose ideas were rejected by the common opinion of the human race. Rendered thus into solemn Latin cadences, the thoughts of Henry George in his *Progress and Poverty* were reduced to their utmost simplicity and rejected out of hand.[6]

The main thrust of the section on the family was an affirmation of its rights as taking precedence over taking those of the State. In the primitive form in which some continental socialism expressed itself at that time, such an affirmation meant that the socialists would appear to want to destroy the family by substituting paternal and maternal care by that of the State and, thereby, advocating a doctrine contrary to natural justice. To want the State to exercise its authority within the intimate circle of the family was judged as a 'gross and pernicious error', except in cases in which the family found itself in great difficulty, or need, or there was a grave disturbance of mutual rights.[7]

The socialists were further berated because they became mere dreamers in wanting perfect equality between all members of the human race. It was clearly 'vain to struggle against the course of nature' which, by giving people differing natural gifts resulted in their attaining differing social conditions and economic status. The ambivalent conclusion was drawn that differing conditions conferred differing rights, but then Volpini partly strengthened and added to the text of the Italian draft. In so doing, he made it plain that he was also a genuine contributor to the sense and content of the overall texts. He wrote, 'The rights of each person are sacred and must be regarded as such. In order that each may hold to what is his, public authority must provide equally by preventing and punishing injury and this is the only equality to which each may fruitfully aspire and rightly claim as his own.'[8]

In his draft, Liberatore had spoken of the duty of the State to be aware of the particular needs of the poor in the protection of their rights. The rich, who are more powerful, are able to look after themselves while the poor, without resources of their own, have no other recourse than to the State. Since the workers, in great part, make up the 'class of the poor' they have especial need of the care and protection of the State. Volpini was careful to make it plain that the role of the State was subsidiary in coming to the aid of the poor.

After having taken pains previously to personalise the socialists and the capitalists, he adopted a different device for the poor and the rich. Liberatore's 'il povero' became 'the mass of the poor' [miserum vulgus] while 'il ricco' became the 'rich class [Natio divitum] and 'the workers who generally belong to the class' of the poor' became 'wage earners who are numbered normally amongst the mass of the needy'. The use of the Latin gave great potency to the argument and also introduced a mild element of class struggle which most of the document tried to play down, without denying the existence of classes. Nevertheless, there was no acceptance of the notion of the classes being locked into an ineluctable struggle.[9]

Volpini, following Liberatore, insisted that earthly life, however good and treasured it may be, was not the final end of the human person, but only a means towards the perfection of the life of the spirit because the person was made in God's image. This led to the further insistence that the life of the spirit was a common possession of every individual because in it 'all men are equals and there is no distinction between rich and poor, master and servant, prince and subject for "the same God is Lord over all".' (Rom. 10: 12) Then followed a statement which was taken almost exactly from Liberatore and which lay at the heart of all Christian social teaching. In essence, it was the key point of Rerum Novarum itself and all papal pronouncements on the social question from 1891 onwards. The equality of all, based on their creation by God is paramount. It is an equality which flows from a form of dependence of the creature on the Creator, and results in an equality without limits because it leads to eternal life.

> *No one may outrage with impunity that human dignity*
> *which God Himself treats with great reverence, or impede in*
> *any way that striving for perfection which is consistent with*
> *eternal life. Moreover, man himself can never renounce his*
> *right to be treated according to his nature and to surrender*
> *himself to any form of slavery of the spirit. In this matter it*
> *is not a question of rights which a man is free to renounce,*
> *but of duties towards God which must be held as sacred.*[10]

In that paragraph the equality of all human beings, based on their creation by God is pronounced without equivocation, but it is from their state of dependence that all else follows. Equality without dependence has no reality while, with it, equality has no limits because it leads to eternal life. In that sense, the paragraph encapsulated the essence of Christian social teaching which stemmed back to Christ himself.

After such a proposition, it is almost puzzling that its immediate translation into the realm of practicality was a section dealing in detail with the hours of rest. Nonetheless, physical rest, given its relationship with the observance of the Sabbath, was close to the heart of men whose primary concern was with worship as a duty towards God. Rest from labour had to be proportionate to the amount of strength used up in work, because such rest was intended to fulfil the need for physical and mental restoration, which clearly differed for women and children. Sunday rest was vigourously enjoined, provided it helped man to turn his thoughts to God rather than to idleness, indulgence and vice. An owner or a worker could not enter into a contract in which rest and restoration were neither expressed nor presupposed, because no one could require or consent to the giving up of those duties which a man owes to himself and to God.[11]

Volpini struggled painfully through the long and tortured passages on wages which Zigliara had elaborated from the pithy statements of Liberatore.[12] Gone was all reference to a necessary, component element for the family being included in the wage, but the new concept of work being both personal and necessary was retained. That work was necessary was clear, because only work enabled a man to procure the means to sustain life. Although the worker and the employer could make free agreements as to the wage paid, even to the extent that a worker could accept less than he was entitled to, or work indeed for nothing if he so wished, there was another necessary element. Natural justice also entered into the contract and regulated the wage based on the place in which the work was done, and the greater or lesser level of the cost of living.

The most important element regulating the wage was that it could not be less than that which was necessary for the sustenance of life in the circumstances in which the worker found himself. Volpini changed this to read: 'an element of natural justice, ancient and superior to the free will of the contracting parties, demands that the wages be sufficient for the sustenance of the worker.' In effect, Volpini must have considered the variable of the cost of living and the place in which the work was done as extraneous to the contract and, in any case, as too nebulous, probably on the well-meaning assumption that such matters would be taken into account in any case. The result was that, without the intervention of the State or the trade unions, a worker would receive exactly what an employer decided to pay him, irrespective of any concept of natural justice flowing from circumstances. Indeed, Liberatore or Zigliara had foreseen precisely what was likely to happen if necessity, or fear of unemployment, forced the workers to suffer unjust violence. The State would have to interfere unduly, which would lead to a kind of State socialism, so that it was better to leave such matters to organisations of a kind with which the encyclical would deal in a later section. In fact, following Liberatore, Zigliara had spoken of corporations composed of owners and workers, which Volpini put as associations without then specifying their composition, but he promised to return to them later.[13]

The next passage, taken from Liberatore's final draft, is notable in that it entirely preempts the question of a just wage in respect of wife and family. What it does is speak of a wage which is sufficient to permit the worker to live with his wife and children *'in una tal quale agiatezza'* [in a certain degree of comfort] which Volpini shortened to *'commodum'* [comfortably]. Such a man, were he sensible, would economise and save in order to acquire a small piece of property. Indeed, his own innate desires would incline him to this end. For Zigliara, as well as Liberatore, the conclusion was that the right to private property is the indispensable, practical and efficacious solution to the worker question and, thus, savings and frugality were the means to achieve that desirable objective of private ownership. Volpini also thought that the worker problem could not be solved except by recognising the principle of private property as sacred and inviolable. He proclaimed the need for the law to favour private ownership and help as many as possible of the multitude of the people to become owners.[14]

The importance of this section lies, firstly, in the fact that the ghost of Liberatore's family wage was firmly laid to rest by removing any vestige of such a requirement from the work contract. That it was a necessity to do so stems essentially from the immense practical problems inherent in the abstract concept of a family wage paid in justice, as much as it does from theological considerations. As a consequence, the Church, through its highest teaching authority, was unable to endorse an obligation in justice on the part of the employers, which could only later be enforced by worker agitation and State intervention. Both eventualities ran counter to the fond hope of the encyclical, with its fear of socialism and State socialism, that some form of amicable co-operation between the employers and the employees would settle such matters favourably. Secondly, by using the idea of worker savings it was possible to canonise the concept of private property.

The original suggestion of a 'small piece of fixed property' had become 'a small piece of property' (*qualche piccola proprieta*) but to Boccali, who looked at this passage closely later, even that was perhaps an exaggeration and he wrote in the margin, 'Isn't that going too far? It is the Pope who is speaking.' Despite his unease, it was rendered into Latin as *'modicum census'* which should be understood at the least as 'a small piece of property' and can be translated as 'a small piece of land'. The census, in Roman times, was the roll of names and assessment of the property of all Roman citizens so that the Latin word 'census', by transference, meant property or wealth and Cicero spoke of a poor man as *'homo sine censu'*. The argument was that the possession of landed property by the generality of workers would help to strike at the heart of the worker question and solve its more intractable problems.[15]

The first good result which would flow from the possession of private property would be a more equitable distribution of goods. The development of industrial capitalism had resulted in the formation of two groups in society and the first was portrayed, in words firmly based on Liberatore, as the faction holding power because it has wealth. Hence it controls all labour and trade, manipulating the source of supply and even exercising great influence in the administration of the State. On the other side, there was that needy and weak multitude of the poor, broken in spirit and therefore ever likely to cause trouble.[16]

By encouraging the workers to look forward to private ownership, the gulf would be lessened between the two classes and they would come closer together. Despite the caution shown in respect of the form of ownership, the Latin text firmly implied that land was one possible form, indeed the most desirable one, of private ownership. It translated the Italian by saying that the productivity of the land would be much greater because men toil harder when working their own soil which they learn to love as it produces food and abundant goods for themselves and their loved ones, adding thereby to both communal and personal wealth. The final fruit of this form of private property would be the curtailment of migration because men would prefer to remain in the land of their birth provided they could there live in decency and happiness.[17]

All this led to a final fling at socialists and even at the shadowy figures of Henry George and Father McGlynn across the Atlantic.

> *It is, however, impossible to achieve these several benefits unless on the condition that private means are not exhausted by the need to pay excessive taxation. The right to possess private property does not flow from the law of man, but from that of nature. Public authority cannot abolish that right, but can only moderate its use and make it harmonise with the common good. The State would act in an unjust and inhumane manner were it to exact more than is just from private owners under the guise of a tax.* [18]

Volpini clearly felt at home with the next section in which the major premise was that 'the remedy for the evils of the workers must come from amongst the workers themselves rather than from the State'. While this was again a stress on lessening State intervention, the more positive response was contained in Volpini's refusal to use the word corporations although he, following Liberatore, cast a glance backward at the old guilds and praised their usefulness. Finally, the big step was taken to break with the past when Volpini, facing the fact that changes had to take place to accommodate the developments in society since the Middle Ages, used the words *'sodalitia opificum'* which clearly meant workers' organisations or trade unions, although he hoped with Liberatore that they would retain the spirit of the old guilds.[19]

At last, the right of the workers to form their own unions was vigorously asserted and defended and the actual organisation of the unions themselves examined with an openness of mind. In particular, their right to have their own existence within the State was set down with firmness and no equivocation. Aquinas had distinguished the public society of the State in which 'Men establish relations in common with one another in the setting up of a commonwealth' from private societies in which citizens come together for their own particular ends.[20]

Although such societies are in some sense part of the totality of the State, it is not permissible for any State to prohibit their existence, because to enter into them is a natural right and it is the duty of the State to encourage the use of natural rights, rather than to impede them. For a State to act against a private society or trade union on the grounds of prohibiting citizens to come together for their own purposes would be to deny the very principle upon which the State itself existed, namely the natural tendency of human beings to come together in society. While a State could forbid the setting up of such associations which it deemed dangerous to its own existence, every care had to be taken to act within right reason and never to impose unjust laws under the pretext of public utility. In effect, the encyclical was using the principle of natural rights of association to delineate the shape of 'civil society' in which autonomous units, operating within the rule of law in the democratic State, would, in pursuit of their own ends, contribute to the well-being of all citizens.

Checks and balances were thereby written into the text that left States in the exact position in which their own existence rightly placed them — they were bound to protect the existence of private associations, including trade unions, on the same principle upon which they protected their own. In asserting such a principle, the encyclical was also rejecting the concept of the State as absolute and omnipotent which Leo, in his encyclical, *Libertas Praestantissimum* of 1888, had already rejected and castigated as a tenet of the kind of liberalism with which the Church in continental Europe was all too familiar.[21]

The remainder of the Italian draft was faithfully translated by Volpini. In the main it dealt with the mission of the Church and, consequently, only in a secondary sense, contributed to the main argument of the encyclical which concentrated on the rights and duties of the workers, the employers and the State. Nevertheless, it forcibly argued that Christianity had brought about a 'social transformation' which marked true progress for the human race. Liberatore had harked back to the primary responsibility of the Church for the poor and the weak in whom she saw the person of Christ. Volpini did him the credit of including those words in the text.[22]

There was no conclusion to Liberatore's final Italian draft, nor did Volpini attempt to include one in his own, which perhaps indicates that he realised he was not to have the last word. His work had taken him ten weeks from 17 November to 31 January 1891. Leo was immediately given the Latin version to read, and clearly, there was some considerable need for haste were the encyclical to be ready for publication in order that it would coincide with May Day, 1891. The Pope read and re-read the Latin text and called Volpini to his study. In his customary nasal drawl Leo said, 'Yes, the material is all there, but it lacks tone.' He made his dissatisfaction plain with a slow and solemn gesture and said, 'You have to throw it all away and begin from the beginning.' Ten weeks work and an impending May Day notwithstanding, Leo was not about to be satisfied with anything he judged to be short of perfection. It was back to the drawing board again for the increasingly exhausted secretaries.[23]

Seven

Issued at Rome

May Day as a goal seemed impossible for the publication of the encyclical, but an attempt still had to be made to meet the deadline which had been set, in hope, more than in reality. That Leo was dissatisfied with more than the tone of Volpini's translation was apparent. Notwithstanding marsala, biscuits and Horace, what the Pope now wanted was a complete reworking in the form of another Italian draft. As such, it was to be the fourth attempt at an Italian draft and the sixth overall attempt which illustrated a great deal of the painstaking approach taken by Leo to the most momentous document of his reign as Pope.

With the intention of retaining Volpini as the final Latin translator, Leo turned to Gabriele Boccali for the reworking of Liberatore's last Italian draft. Boccali was regarded in the Vatican as the chief interpreter of the Pope when it came to expressing his thoughts in written form. In the event, Boccali clarified some parts of the text, rearranged others, wrote an introduction and a conclusion, but the overall sense of the encyclical was preserved, and he added little of moment to it. As only three manuscript pages have survived, it has to be judged by Volpini's further attempt at a Latin version which, in the event, proved to be the last one done prior to the final and official retouching.[1]

The first contribution of Boccali was substantial. From long-established custom, he knew that the actual title of the encyclical would come from his opening sentence and, furthermore, that the whole tenor of the document would be set by its opening paragraph. From it, later readers and commentators would judge, in part at least, the overall trend of the encyclical so that it behoved him to get it right. He stuck to the heading which Liberatore had given to the very first Italian version, *'La Questione Operaia'* and then, after three attempts he finally settled on a form of words which he thought suitable to begin his sentence. *'Le gravi agitazioni e turbamenti che travagliono da tempo la presente societa . . .'* (The serious agitations and commotions which for so long have distressed modern society . . .[2]

When Volpini came to translate that sentence for the Latin version he began with *'Excitata semel rerum novarum cupidine, quae diu commovet civitates . . .'* (Once enkindled, the burning desire for change which for so long has been stirring up the masses . . .'). After much thought, he decided to vary the opening line as he, more than Boccali, knew that the title of the encyclical would be his. With a happy *coup de plume* he simply switched the sentence so that it began with the words *'Rerum novarum'* which became the title of the encyclical and under which it has passed to posterity.[3]

The difficulty with the decision to begin the encyclical with the words *'Rerum Novarum'* was that they did not render the sense of the Italian, once taken in their Latin contextual background. That very phrase *'rerum novarum cupidus'* was often used by Roman authors of the late Republic and always in a derogatory sense, whether of persons or of the people, or, more appropriately, the 'mob'. Cicero, Caesar and Sallust had used it in that sense. As a result it was commonly taken to mean that the people or the 'mob' were often stirred up by their desire to overthrow the existing order, and in that way it was understood by students of the late Republic.

The official version in Italian, which was printed in *L'Osservatore Romano* on 23 May 1891, translated the opening sentence in a way that made it conform to the sense of the old Latin authors. 'L'ardente brama di novità, che da gran tempo ha incominciato ad agitare i popoli' (The burning desire for change, which for so long has begun to stir up the masses) makes this plain.[4] But, disregarding the classical interpretation of the

Latin, the true text simply meant that once the desire for change, which for a long time had been disturbing people, had been awakened it eventually had to manifest itself in the social and economic spheres as well as in politics.

It is understandable that the earliest English translators would read the opening words in their classical context and hence render the first paragraph as:

> *That the spirit of revolutionary change which has long been disturbing the nations of the world, should have passed beyond the sphere of politics and made its influence felt in the cognate sphere of practical economics is not surprising.*[5]

The very use of the words ' revolutionary change' conjured up visions of violence and bloodshed which, over time , had found their source and cause in movements alien to the Church. As a consequence, it was easy, especially were one not inclined to read and think about the whole text, to see the encyclical as 'the Church's complete answer to *Das Kapital* of Marx, and, indeed, to Communism and Socialism in whatever forms'.[6]

No one could deny that, for over a hundred years, changes of a radical kind had been troubling people all around the industrialised and semi-industrialised world. Nonetheless, the important source from which they stemmed, and which lay at the critical core of the encyclical, was the grim results of the industrial capitalism of the nineteenth century which J.S. Mill had criticised in its baneful manifestations and Dickens had exposed. Then or later, to caricature the encyclical by a free translation of its first line as merely another papal condemnation of socialism was to cast a gloss on its meaning which Leo never intended, despite the trenchant criticism of socialism which it contained.

Throughout *Rerum Novarum*, by his own positive choice, Leo was addressing himself to the problems confronted by the working masses. In fact, Boccali had gone on to state without equivocation, and Volpini had even strengthened his meaning, that the current painful vicissitudes had their origins in the changes that had taken place in the relationship between masters and their workers, in the great wealth amassed by a few and the extreme poverty of so many workers. To Leo, many owners were greedy speculators who were using human beings as mere instruments in their pursuit of profits.

The Pope went on to grieve 'that little by little the workers have been abandoned and left without defence. They find themselves at the mercy of greedy employers and a system of unrestrained competition. To this situation must be added the evil of rapacious usury which, although condemned so often by the Church, nonetheless with like injustice is still practised by covetous and grasping men under other forms . . .'. In ringing tones he deplored the fact that 'a monopoly of production and commerce has fallen into the hands of a small number of tycoons who have laid upon the teeming masses of the labouring poor a yoke little better than slavery itself'. Finally, he insisted that the most important instrument in the hands of the workers was the trades union.[7]

Leo was concerned with socialism, but as an effect of industrial capitalism. Assuredly, he deplored its rejection of private property, together with its notion that 'class is naturally hostile to class' because he believed 'capital cannot do without labour, nor labour without capital'. Yet, the essential conflict arose because capitalism lacked proper control and its deformities were giving the socialists an opportunity to try to stir up the poor to revolt, thus deluding them into thinking that all their problems could be solved by overthrowing the social order. He insisted that 'Nothing is more useful than to look upon the world as it really is . . .'[8] It was unjust that, when Leo did look out upon the world and saw the burdens carried by the under-privileged and the poor, he would be criticised for having seen the reason for so much suffering lying uniquely at the door of the socialists.

Volpini again worked tirelessly so that, by 10 May, he had his Latin version completed, but, even then, Leo was not satisfied.

He had agreed with Boccali about eliminating a large section of three hundred and eighty-five lines from the concluding material, which included a strong rejection of socialism, while the rest dealt with the work of the Church in the social order, but he was still uneasy.[9]

Leo showed the text to others, among whom Cardinal Guiseppe D'Annibale pronounced a favourable opinion while retaining some reservations about that part of the encyclical which dealt with the question of a just wage. Notwithstanding the work already undertaken, Volpini went through again, making small textual and grammatical changes here and there. Leo himself very probably became heavily engaged in all that activity because he practically suspended his papal audiences from 7 to 21 May, with only four held in that time, and he began to hold them again regularly on 22 May.

Finally, the indefatigable Latinist, hopefully having been refreshed from time to time with a glass of marsala and biscuits, was able to write on the cover of the final proof pages '15 *Maggio* 1891', while at the bottom of the frontispiece appears the simple inscription in pen, 'M. Volpini'.[10]

It was now over a year since Father Liberatore had begun work on the first Italian draft. Since then, the text had been through seven, possibly eight, versions, and it ought to have been an immense relief to all concerned when Leo finally permitted the printing of the concluding words on the version held in the Vatican Archives, *'Datum Romae apud S. Petrum die XV Maii An. MDCCCXCI Pontificatus Nostri Decimoquarto Leo P.P. XIII'* (Given at St Peter's, Rome, on 15 May 1891 in the fourteenth year of our Ponificate. Pope Leo XIII.'

It is a testimony to the infinite patience of Monsignor Antonazzi, and proof, if any be needed, that he stood in a long line of men to whom perfection was the ultimate goal, that he was able to observe that, in the official version published in the *Acta Apostolicae Sedis*, the *An.* was changed to *Anno*. He suggested that it was probably done to prevent any unaware reader from reading *An.* as an abbreviation of *Anni* which would not have accorded with the ablative case of *Decimoquarto*.[11] So much for what some call pedantry. Others see it as an ultimate act of serious scholarship and, to that degree, Antonazzi paid his tribute to all those who had worked on the encyclical, none of whom, but especially Leo, was prepared to accept the shoddy or the second-rate.

Even at that late stage, the work was not over. On 17 May *L'Osservatore Romano* published a summary of the encyclical in Italian, promising to put out the Latin text in the following week. It appeared in fact on 19, 20 and 21 May, which also may help explain Leo's lack of public activity on those days. Meanwhile, others retained an interest in the fate of the encyclical and, not the least, Liberatore whose word had been the first. In an impish fashion, and with the privileged position that his years of loyal service accorded him, he was determined to have some say at the end. The *Civiltà Cattolica* had already published the official Latin and Italian texts on 25 May and 8 June. On 22 June, an article by Liberatore appeared in which he said that 'in order to imprint [the encyclical] better in the minds of readers, we will give a kind of paraphrase of it.' To do so, he proceeded to ignore the official versions and went back to the third Italian text of which he, as with the very first, had been the principal author. As Antonazzi rightly states, it confirmed his authorship, although he was careful to avoid offending Leo by otherwise making it public that he had collaborated on the encyclical.[12]

The appearance of the long-awaited encyclical was greeted with varying degrees of enthusiasm. The first American response came from Gibbons. He acknowledged receipt of the encyclical, which he had received from Manning in the English translation, and he had taken it upon himself to send it to the newspapers, to all the American bishops and to the English-speaking bishops in Canada. Gibbons was certain that *Rerum Novarum* would be of particular importance in the United States where, because of the enormous power of capital, the workers felt the greatest need to form unions. After an enigmatic remark which seemed to indicate that he was pleased by the condemnation of Henry George's theories — a remark of variance with his previous attitude, he went on to say that he had long hoped that Leo 'would give us on these matters a positive and explicit teaching . . . My desire has been fulfilled.'[13]

Understandably, Archbishop Corrigan in New York, saw the encyclical in an even more personalised light, given his long involvement with Father McGlynn. Writing to Cardinal Simeoni at Propaganda Fide, he acknowledged that he had always been given strong support by Rome in his own stand for justice and the right to private property and, especially, that to land. He had always thought that such a stand was essential because of the influence of McGlynn, 'a priest little faithful to his duty' coupled with the need to 'repress in the first instance socialist ideas and especially the new theories of Henry George'. Corrigan continued with a singularly inappropriate lack of understanding of the true burden of the encyclical,

> *I am now delighted that the Holy Father has, with the Encyclical on the workers' question, removed every doubt and reassured good Catholics . . . the Holy Father can be happy in having given society great comfort by expressly repudiating certain opinions . . .dangerous to public security and social tranquillity.*[14]

Charles Ward, a self-proclaimed Protestant, wrote to tell Leo that many people in the United States who were not Catholics had, nonetheless, shown their gratitude for an encyclical by which Leo had proved to everyone 'what a true Shepherd should be' but apart from that, little American reaction found its way to Rome.[15]

Despite the encyclical — in fact, as a result of it — the reality of Henry George would not go away. He quickly went into print with *An Open Letter to Pope Leo XIII* when he read *Rerum Novarum*. He rejected its teaching on the private ownership of land and also condemned Leo's acceptance of a natural order of things in which the rich are set aside from the poor and are expected to be charitable to them. His analysis stemmed from his own conviction of the need for a single tax on land and what, over the years, had become almost an obsession with him in comparing the private ownership of land with slavery.[16]

There was no public reaction from the Vatican to the response from George to the encyclical, but three years later, according to Archbishop Ireland of St Paul, Minnesota, Corrigan and some Jesuits were still trying to have the works of George publicly condemned. To Ireland, their pursuit was all a personal matter from which they were determined to emerge victorious. He wrote in alarm to Rampolla as he had heard that Rome was again about to strike at George. He pleaded that *Rerum Novarum* itself was a sufficiently full statement on Catholic teaching on the economic question. Although he personally did not agree with George in respect of a tax on land, he couldn't see how the Church had a right to enter into the question and, as for land held as private property, he thought the matter was not at stake. 'In any case, it is a question that has always been well resolved by the American people', wrote Ireland, which was a reminder to Rome that the alienation of virgin lands in new countries was a different matter to the possession of land in the old world.

He also had a gentle reminder to Rome of the application of standards in the area of free expression of ideas. Any condemnation of George's theories would cause serious trouble in that it would be seen as personal. Americans, stated Ireland, were imbued with very large ideas on the freedom a writer ought to enjoy and to condemn George's work would be seen as an attack on George himself. He concluded with the warning that George's pen used frequently in the past in freely praising the Church and the Pope, could be turned so readily into an attack and, therefore, it would be better to let the matter well alone, despite Corrigan and his Jesuit collaborators.

As was expected, the most relevant reaction to the publication of the encyclical came from those parts of Europe where the conviction was widespread that the concerns which they had expressed to Rome over the preceding years had at last borne fruit. It was a conviction that, then or later, did not bear refutation. The fact that some modest stimulus to the actual timing of the document, as well as a certain tone to the way in which it upheld the right to private property, stemmed from concern with the stand of Henry George and Father McGlynn did nothing to lessen the European contribution to *Rerum Novarum*. The Catholic Congresses, the elaboration of theorists, the speculation on a just wage, the pilgrimages of workers to Rome and the spectacular rise of the socialist movement were all European phenomena, as was Karl Marx himself. Europe, therefore, was the heartland to which the encyclical was addressed and, from Europe, a veritable flood of correspondence poured into the Vatican after its publication.

The general feeling was that, as the social question was 'agitating the whole world' and had 'long awaited an urgent solution', *Rerum Novarum* was, if anything, overdue, although no one was prepared to say so bluntly. The Bishop of Vannes said that Leo had taken the role of 'arbiter in this grave and universal debate upon which depends the tranquillity and happiness of all people'.[17] Charles Phillip Place, Cardinal Archbishop of Rennes, thought the publication of the encyclical was 'one of the most significant events of our century' and 'the charter of a true social economy'. More especially, Place was delighted that Leo had been able to write 'without being preoccupied with school, party or system', by which he meant the theoretical debates that had long plagued the Catholic activists in Europe. He believed it was absolutely essential and urgent to put an end to that 'frightful misunderstanding' which inclined the poor and the workers to see the Church as their enemy.

Place wrote that, with his condemnation of the 'slavelike yoke' that had been imposed on the workers, the Pope had taken a step in that direction, but it had to be remembered that others had got into the front lines and, by their demands for a more humane and equitable organisation of labour relations, they had tried to help the workers and protect them against abuse and injustice. Clearly, Place had in mind the trade unions and, in particular, the socialist trade unions which were already deeply involved in confronting the worker problem and, by implication, he implied that the Church had been left far behind. Whether he also implied that the role of the Church could not be other than in the area of principles, with exhortations to the laity to act in the public sphere, was not made clear. In any case, Rampolla replied in Leo's name to say that the Pope was happy because Place's letter gave substance to the hope that the encyclical would have salutary effects which would work to the benefit of the 'working classes'.[18]

The Queen Regent of Spain sent her thanks and the President of the Spanish Council stated that he wanted the whole nation to conform to the 'primordial and fundamental' ideas contained in the encyclical. In Madrid, the Papal Nuncio quickly had it translated into Spanish and oversaw its distribution among the people, while in Warsaw, the same had happened by 8 June with a Polish translation.[19]

The old Italian sociologist of great fame, Toniolo, quietly rejoiced in Padua, but he remained firm on the corporatist ideal and continued to press for its implementation in later years despite the lack of enthusiasm for it in the encyclical. Professor Helleputte, foremost figure of the Belgian social movement and founder, in 1891, of the Belgian Democratic League was more enthusiastic. As leader of the co-operative societies in that country he said that the encyclical signalled 'the triumph of co-operation' which hardly did justice to the way in which the encyclical had put such matters in their historical context by relinquishing the dream of a revival of the guilds of the past.

In Germany, the encyclical was seen as providing great impetus to the Antisocialist Workers' Federation, while in France the old guard, Breda, Guerin, La Tour du Pin, Henri Lorin and others said that to them it was a precious document which they had awaited with 'confident impatience'. They reminded Leo of their twenty years work as Christian sociologists which was perhaps a way of saying that much of the material contained in the new encyclical had been spelt out by them during those two decades.[20]

Unsurprisingly, some saw the encyclical with partisan eyes. The German Centre had long shared the alarm of many Europeans on the involvement of the State in the 'worker question'; which, to its members, was a form of creeping State socialism. They thought that Leo had cleared up the question splendidly. As a consequence, no fears about the State need be entertained were his guidelines followed, and that was something for which all Germans had reason to be grateful. The Catholic University of Lille had daily expected the encyclical and, as the centre of the industrial north, they saw it as responding to the ever-increasing conflict between 'capital and labour', although they pointed out that there were workplaces where the problem did not exist because the precepts of 'justice and charity' already reigned in them. The workers of Rheims thanked Leo for vindicating their rights, while Antoine Blum and others, representing Swiss workers and sociologists, were delighted that the efficacy of workers, banding together in their own organisations so as to bring about social reform, was recognised by the highest ecclesiastical authority. The Bishop of Rodez and Vabres thought that Leo had done for social theology what Trent had done for moral and dogmatic theology. He was wide of the mark because *Rerum Novarum* looked to the future to chart the course of the Church in the perils of the present age while Trent had looked to the past, in large measure, for its guidelines.[21]

Across the Channel, Manning, as one of the last acts of his long episcopate, wrote an article in the *Dublin Review* in July, 1891. Leo had sent him word of the coming encyclical, as was fitting in respect of one who had so valiantly and for so long defended the working masses and who, in his old age, had won widespread admiration for his support of the London dockworkers in the Great Strike of 1889. Manning recognised that no pope before Leo could have written *Rerum Novarum*, 'for never till now has the world of labour been so consciously united, so dependent upon the will of the rich, so exposed to the fluctuations of adversity and to the vicissitudes of trade'. He said that Leo, during his episcopate at Perugia, had issued even stronger pastorals which were more explicit on the sufferings of the workers and their exploitation by employers, but he took pains to highlight in *Rerum Novarum* the passages that defended the workers, 'given over, isolated and defenceless, to the callousness of employers and the greed of unrestrained capitalism'.

With scarcely concealed contempt, he castigated the warped judgements and obscurantist prejudices of men swayed by ignorance, selfish interests or class feelings. To Manning, such people were the ones who would brand as a socialist anyone trying to protect the workers from the oppression of 'free contracts' or 'starvation wages', when, in reality, all, they wanted to achieve was the isolation of the workers, their dependence on capitalists and their forced labour as an alternative to starvation. So anxious was Manning to see the best in the encyclical that he stated that it defined 'a minimum wage as one sufficient to maintain a man and his home' without going himself into the question as to whether such a wage was based on charity or justice which, he well knew, was the nub of the matter. Overall, his testimony to *Rerum Novarum* was a heartfelt tribute to the cause of the workers from the pen of one who could lay it down in peace.[22]

In the light of Manning's response, it was unfortunate that England made any further reply to the encyclical, but Herbert Vaughan, bishop of Salford, did so on behalf of the Catholic Truth Society, in the form of an address which was acclaimed with much enthusiasm at Westminster Town Hall in early July 1891. The address was mostly a series of platitudes, rendered even less sensible by a rerun of the annual wail of lament summed up by Vaughan as 'the infamous and sacrilegious spoliation of the Holy See at the hand of the Italian revolution'.[23] Vaughan's response had as little meat to it as most of the flood of telegrams which greeted the encyclical from all parts of Europe, but one from the Società Operaia La Romanina used an expression of Leo which must have given joy to the old Pope because it called him 'Father of the Workers'. He may have wondered about the full meaning of the letter from Marie François Carnot, President of the French Republic, who thanked him profusely on behalf of that 'peaceful working democracy' which France had become in the nineteenth century, but it was a gracious tribute nonetheless.[24]

When Michael Logue, Primate of All Ireland, replied on behalf of the Irish bishops, he did little but rejoice that the errors of the socialists and the perverse doctrine of the communists had been rejected, the right of private owners upheld, the oppressors of the poor confused and hope held out to the workers and those who were miserable.[25] Some of those who were closer to the people than the bishops, such as three former students of Propaganda Fide College who wrote to the Cardinal Prefect in Rome, were conscious that, in Ireland, many tenant farmers lived in fear of being expelled from their homes by 'cruel and unjust' owners. One of them said that, because the Church seemed to favour the rich and the powerful many of the Irish poor and dispossessed regarded the bishops as 'pastors who have left their flocks to the mercy of a wolf'. In April 1888, Leo had allowed the Holy Office to issue a decree which was mostly condemnatory of Irish agrarian agitation so that he had become 'for the immense majority of the people not much more than a Judas'. As a consequence, an encyclical letter that gave no weight to the rights of agricultural labourers and tenants in danger of losing their means of sustenance was unlikely to arouse much of a response in Ireland.[26]

In distant Australia, a somewhat depressing note was struck at first. Cardinal Moran, Archbishop of Sydney, rejoiced in the Roman purple as his country's first cardinal. He saw a cable report on the publication of *Rerum Novarum* and wrote to his Roman agent, Monsignor Kirby, Rector of the Irish College: 'I think they ought to send me an official copy of such important documents before they are given to the newspapers. It is rather strange for a cardinal to have to say that he knows nothing of the matter, except that it was reported by the public press.'

In fact, Kirby had already anticipated Moran and, twelve days before, he had written to Sydney in more triumphal tones, as befitted his closeness to the Roman scene. 'I sent Y.E. [Your Eminence] the late grand enciclical [sic] of H.H. [His Holiness] on the labour question. It has excited the universal admiration of all Europe. The Spanish government has announced its intention to make it the basis of their future legislation on the question which may affect the relations between capitalists and the operatives.' Clearly, Kirby had taken the trouble to read the encyclical and to have an understanding of its contents.[27]

No other response seems to have been evident from Sydney in 1891, but that from Melbourne was more ebullient. The normally kindly and urbane Archbishop Carr had alienated a substantial group of Catholics in 1890 during a series of strikes in his city. In a circular which reached Propaganda Fide in Rome, they accused him of taking money from the workers and then doing nothing to ameliorate their condition when they 'conscientiously abstain from work until the employers will listen to reason, justice and common sense'. They reserved their praise for Cardinal Manning in London and for the Victorian Chief Justice, George Higinbotham, 'who has thrown himself heart and soul into the cause of the Union'. Perhaps some of their criticism explained the alacrity with which Carr responded to *Rerum Novarum* for, by 13 July 1891, he had written to Propaganda to say that he had caused the document to be read in all the churches of his archdiocese so as to bring it to the notice of all the faithful. He was proud to say that it had been received '*maxima cum reverentia*' by both the workers and the employers.[28]

The support which Manning had given during the London dock strikes to the workers was well known in Australia, and the workers' movement in that country had subscribed considerable sums of money to support their London counterparts. In 1893, portraits of Higinbotham and Manning, commissioned by the workers of Ballarat, were unveiled in their Trades Hall. One speaker eulogised Manning as 'the greatest reformer of the present century' while, to another, Higinbotham was 'Australia's greatest dead', and a third said that the two 'were the greatest advocates of justice for the toilers of the present age'.[29]

Three priests, former students of Propaganda Fide College in Rome, wrote from their parishes in Australia to say how well the encyclical had been received and one, Frank O'Gorman, of Newcastle, asserted that, in no other country on earth, had it occasioned more joy 'amongst Catholics and Protestants of all classes' which was surely a grotesque exaggeration.[30] In the Vatican, and, more particularly, in the Secretariat of State, the enthusiastic reply from Australia caused no comment and, indeed, some people working there were unsure of what actually made up the continent. A gentleman named Hahnemann Rogers of Tapu Thamas, New Zealand clearly thought the main burden of the encyclical was anti-socialist, and he wrote a disjointed letter to Leo giving what he called the socialist answer to *Rerum Novarum*. On it, someone in the Secretariat of State wrote, 'The reply of an Australian socialist to the encyclical on the social question'.[31]

There is a last word which needs to be added, although it predated *Rerum Novarum* by three years. In 1888, Archbishop Corrigan had already written the first phrase of the encyclical when he wrote to Rome to tell Propaganda Fide that one of his priests was *'Rerum novarum cupidus, atque opinionum singularium sectator* — a priest 'who longed for revolutionary change and who was a follower of singular opinions'. The priest in question, Edward MacSweeney was, like McGlynn, an ex-alumnus of Propaganda College, Rome. MacSweeney, to the end, defended his old friend of college days because, to him, McGlynn was 'another Christ' who had never offended in chastity, temperance and obedience.[32] Thus New York, the Vatican and the late Roman Republic were bound up in the first line of the encyclical. Any individual, or the 'mob' itself, who posed a threat to entrenched positions of power was seen as bent on revolution. Nonetheless, it was far from Leo's mind to condemn the working masses as revolutionaries when he let the encyclical go out with its title open to that inflammatory implication.

Eight

Acceptance and Rejection

During the long gestation period of *Rerum Novarum*, there was time, among European Catholics at least, to develop concepts on the 'social question' in areas which needed clarification because they had caused conflict. The question of State intervention was one such matter and agreement had been reached, at least tacitly, on it. No one any longer rejected, out of hand, the need for the State to intervene on behalf of the common good of the workers in the relations between capital and labour. Action by the State was sometimes imperative and its general involvement was agreed upon, provided the limits of its function were carefully delineated, and the encyclical itself took that stance strongly. Thus, with the matter of State intervention apparently settled, the one that remained was even thornier because it went to the core of the concept of justice. The question of a just wage had long agitated European theorists and it was of immediate and pressing interest to see what Leo had made of it.

For eighty years, no one was privy to how Liberatore had treated the question in his first draft. In it, he had insisted that a just wage had to include an element which permitted a worker to provide for his wife and family, as well as for himself. As the encyclical moved from draft to draft, that principle was weakened to the degree that it appeared impossible to assert, on reading the propositions contained in the text, that a family wage had its basis in justice. Nevertheless, the encyclical, in essence, said that injustice was not necessarily avoided merely because a worker consented with apparent freedom to a wage contract. The encyclical carefully stated that human labour is both personal, in that it belongs to the one who does it, and necessary, because, without it life cannot be sustained. From this, it follows that 'each one has a natural right to procure what is required in order to live, and the poor can achieve that end in no other way than by what they earn through their work'.[1]

Nonetheless, free agreements between capital and labour were accepted as the norm, provided they were underpinned by 'a dictate of natural justice greater and more ancient than any free contract, namely that remuneration ought to be sufficient to support a frugal and well-behaved wage earner'.[2] Despite this, there is no mention of family, nor can it be implied that natural justice demands more from the employer than that he pays what a prudent worker needs for his own support.

The next paragraph certainly goes on to say that, if a worker is paid a wage 'sufficient to enable him to maintain himself, his wife and his children in reasonable comfort', he ought to behave sensibly, make economies, save and thereby accrue enough capital to secure a small piece of property which would be something that his own innate desires would incline him towards.[3] In short, while implying the relationship between the worker and his family, the fact remains that the encyclical nowhere stated that justice obliged an employer to pay a wage which took into account the need of the worker to provide for his family as well as himself.

Understandably, there was immediate concern as to the exact meaning of the encyclical on the question of a just wage. The most important and weighty intervention came from Cardinal Goosens, Archbishop of Malines. It was the eve of a Congress to be held in his city and he was certain that the matter would come forward, possibly causing divisions among those in attendance and perhaps even acrimonious interchanges and resulting confusion. Clearly, he was also concerned that such an eventuality might tend to weaken the support for the encyclical. On 10 August 1891, he wrote to Rome, posing three precise questions which, in Latin, allowed him to use terminology familiar to the Vatican experts, but, more importantly, to reveal the complexity of the matter. In essence, he asked:

1. Does natural justice, as used in the encyclical in reference to a just wage, mean the same as commutative justice?
2. Does an employer sin if he pays enough for the sustenance of the worker, but not for his wife and children? If the answer is in the affirmative, against what virtue does he sin?
3. Whether, and for what reason, an employer sins who, without using force or fear, but because of a depressed labour market, pays a wage which is less than the work done merits and is insufficient for reasonable sustenance, but to which the worker nonetheless consents.[4]

Those questions, simple and uncomplicated as they seemed, went to the heart of the matter, although they ignored the complicated matter of recurring trade cycles which had to affect wages. If natural justice was to be read as commutative justice, which governs the rights that exist as between one individual and another, then an employer would sin gravely were he to pay less than the sum to which an employee was entitled based on the value of the work done. Furthermore, the employer in those circumstances would be bound to restitution, and, in the event that he did not do so, the worker could engage in hidden compensation to make up the difference. The second question addressed itself to the concept of a family wage and attacked squarely the problem of whether justice required its payment or merely charity. The third raised the problem of free consent. It had long been established that workers were free to sell their labour, provided the employer used no fraud or force to induce them to do so. But what if the state of the labour market was such that, in desperation, workers offered themselves willingly for a wage that was less than their due? In a depressed economy, with unemployment and bankruptcies rife, such a state of affairs could easily arise.

Both Leo and Goosens knew that the questions were put in the context of arguments between respectable theologians. To illustrate that point, Goosens cited De Lugo as one who had held that a wage need not necessarily be unjust if it were insufficient for the upkeep of a wife and children, nor indeed insufficient for the maintenance of a worker himself.[5] The result was that Goosens' questions had to be given very serious consideration in the Vatican and, when Cardinal Rampolla discussed the matter with Leo, it was decided that an authoritative opinion was needed.

Clearly, it was difficult to turn to Liberatore as the authority because he had already shown bias, at least to the extent that he regarded a family wage as a matter of justice. Equally clearly, Cardinal Zigliara had shown bias, but it was in another direction and one which all reason indicated was right, as the whole history of this vexed question had proven from the very earliest days when it had come up for discussion amongst theologians and at Congresses. In any case, Zigliara was asked to formulate an answer in his capacity as Prefect of the Sacred Congregation of Studies.[6]

The replies, as preserved in the Vatican Archives are in Latin and French. There is a lengthy explanation with each answer, but no hint is given that they came from Zigliara. The answer to the first question was very precise. Natural justice had to be read as commutative justice which meant that a just wage was one in which there was an inherent and exact balance between the wage paid and the work done. Justice was therefore violated if the employer paid less than the due wage, or if the worker did less than the due work. The reply on a family wage was again simple in that it affirmed that such was not due in justice, but that an employer who refused to pay it could sometimes sin against charity or natural honesty.

Zigliara spelled out, in full, the reason for his answer. Work was a personal thing which was done by the worker and not by his family. Therefore, it was not directed to the benefit of his family in the first instance, but only secondarily. The distinction was neat, but it went far beyond mere playing with words. No hard and fast rules on the moral plane were established, but the ultimate resolution of the matter was left to the participants in the work contract or, failing that, to public authority, to determine whether a component element for the needs of the family would be included in the wage paid. In 1891, the concept of social justice was little more than a ray on the distant horizon and the task of *Rerum Novarum* was to lay down guidelines which, hopefully, would, over time, lead to that light. Clear as it later became that the horizon of social justice always appeared distant, the strength of the encyclical lay exactly in the fact that it did not run ahead of its time and cause confusion by confounding the real with the ideal.

The third question was entirely practical because everyone knew that, especially in times of economic recession with accompanying unemployment, workers readily grasped at jobs in which they were paid less than their due. In Italy itself, the case was apparent. Landless labourers worked up to seventeen hours in summer for very low wages and, as the nineteenth century went on, wages were becoming lower and there were always more hands available than jobs. Thus competition was extremely keen and workers vied with each other for employment, with the result that employers could fix wage rates as low as workers would accept them.

The Vatican's reply to the question was very clear. In such cases, employers sinned against commutative justice because the wage they paid was unjust. Zigliara used an unhappy analogy in reverse to make his point. A seller who sold goods at a higher price than they warranted sinned against justice. Equally, the employer who bought labour at a lower price than it warranted sinned against justice. The analogy limped because, in a glutted market, sellers are often forced to offload their products at lower prices than they warranted, just as workers had to sell their labour at a lower price in similar circumstances. He would have been on safer grounds by sticking to the essential point about human labour, made so strongly in the encyclical, that it could not be compared to the buying and selling of goods exactly because it was an extension of the human person involving his rights and his dignity.[7]

Nonetheless, with the clear and unequivocal answer based on justice, a point was made forcibly which, if acted upon, would have restrained capitalism in those circumstances in which it was based on excessive profits or sweated labour. At the very least, it would have impeded the progress of capitalism by removing from its midst that portion of its profits stemming from unjust wages paid by Catholic employers who, in Europe at least, were constantly increasing in numbers.

Regrettably, given the clarity of the replies or, indeed, perhaps because they were so clear, there were some misgivings in the Vatican about the appropriate manner of their promulgation. Goosens wanted to state publicly that he had proposed the questions to the Pope for resolution. He sent a suggested introduction in French to Rome which said that he had put the questions to Leo and that he had received the answers through Rampolla. There is a black, wavering line in ink alongside Goosens' introduction which looks very much like the symbol used by Leo when he wanted material reconsidered. In the event, Zigliara advised that the replies should be published as coming from a consultant rather than from the Pope and Leo agreed with him that the matter of publication should be handled in that way. Rampolla therefore told Goosens not to say that Leo had been asked to clarify the matters raised but merely that 'given the gravity and delicacy of the argument, a consultant had been engaged to examine the doubts raised and give his opinion on them'. This tortured way of proceeding elicited a compromise from Goosens. Instead of saying that Leo had been approached directly, he would say that he had proposed certain doubts to the Holy See which had asked a consultant to reply.[8]

The solution arrived at was neat enough in that it did not commit Leo directly, so that no one could say that the Pope had given an explicit directive on the matters raised. In that way, the consciences of Catholic employers and their ecclesiastical directors would seem to be salved in circumstances where an explicit papal pronouncement was lacking. On the other hand, some strength would also be given to the progressives who could rightly state that the Holy See had taken their part. In consequence, both sides could feel justified. In the event, Goosens did not publish the replies at all and it was not until 22 March 1892 that they appeared publicly, and then only at the hands of Father Esbach in *Science catholique*.[9] The whole episode served to illustrate how difficult it was for the Church to deal with the increasing world of Catholic capitalism which still retained its powerful influence through and after the days of *Rerum Novarum*. The encyclical was not premature, but the wonder is that it was not stillborn.

No one expected that *Rerum Novarum* would be accepted with passivity in all quarters. Its very subtitle, 'The Condition of the Working Classes', as the English translation put it rather than the more direct Italian 'The Worker Question', was still sufficiently suggestive to swing the emphasis of the Church's social teaching in a direction that caused unease to many. Cautious though its phraseology was in most parts, the ringing condemnation of contemporary capitalism and its forms gave pause for thought to those whose increasing material wellbeing depended upon the maintenance and continued strengthening of such a system. The fundamental proposition that a solution to the ills of society which ignored the Church would be futile, was as useful a rejection of militant socialism as any number of condemnations of individual facets of socialism such as a constant reiteration of the teaching on private property.

Equally, the insistence throughout *Rerum Novarum* on the need for the State to intervene in designated areas, and for the requirement that Church and State co-operate to help solve the 'worker question', was anathema to those secularists who held that the Church had no role to play in public affairs. It was equally unacceptable to those traditionalist Catholics who rejected the role of the State in so-called private matters. Finally, the fact that the Pope had spoken on the 'social question' was, to some, a stumbling block, to others, a ray of hope, and for many, a source of confusion. Those who looked upon the papacy as the last vestige of medieval clericalism were brought up short, for whatever else it was, the document, if read at all fairly, was neither obscurantist nor mean-souled. On the other hand, the appeal to those to whom Peter spoke through Leo was potent in that the poor, the disadvantaged and the oppressed were the subjects of page after page in the encyclical. That, in itself, was a noble return to the New Testament, from which the whole edifice of the Church claimed its historical and theological reason for being.

Reverberations of unrest were quickly heard, even within the Catholic world itself. Charles Francis Juring was bishop of Nancy in France. His See, although small, was traditionally strongly Catholic and the bishop was a powerful figure. Shortly after the publication of the encyclical he issued a pastoral letter of his own. According to Cardinal Langenieux, Archbishop of Rheims, the pastoral stirred up very considerable reaction in both France and Belgium. In his judgement it was no less than a polemic directed against Albert De Mun and his school, and formed part of a sustained attack which the Bishop had mounted over some years against progressive circles within European Catholicism. Yet, wrote the Cardinal, the very people under attack by the Bishop, were the same ones who had always been in accord with Leo and, in some senses, they had even anticipated him in his teachings on the 'social question'.

In the Vatican, it was known that Langenieux was an outspoken and courageous defender of De Mun and, together with Leon Harmel, they had led the pilgrimage to Rome of 2,000 workers in 1887 on which occasion both he and De Mun had spoken before Leo and the papal court. Langenieux was puzzled as to how he ought to act in the matter, as he did not want to enter the lists publicly with a bishop, but he clearly felt that some sort of action was necessary, either to refute or to silence him. Rampolla showed the letter to Leo who agreed that there be no public reply to Juring and they decided that the best course was for Langenieux to get in touch with the Papal Nuncio in Paris who would advise him on the matter.[10]

In the meantime, Juring himself had also written to Rampolla. He was thrown into a frenzy of denunciatory prose because a certain Father de Pascal had published a pamphlet refuting Juring's pastoral letter. He told Rampolla that some Catholics were using the encyclical to bolster their own 'inexact and erroneous doctrines on property', but he did not spell out their errors. Even worse, they were doing all possible to foster the spread of the *Association Catholique de la Jeunesse Francaise*. The purpose of the Association, according to Juring, was to propagate among young people, doctrines which were opposed to papal teaching, and it served only to further the obstinacy and ambition of De Mun. Some months beforehand, a bishop had said to Juring that De Mun's school was 'a sect in process of formation' while an archbishop had remarked to him that, 'If De Mun isn't stopped by direct action now, there will be no stopping him.'

De Mun and his circle, according to Juring, had one purpose. They wanted to train up politicians who would engage in party political activity to the detriment of the Church, and De Mun had used, and was using, every possible means to that end. Juring said that he had drawn Leo's attention to all these matters two years previously, giving proof of his assertions, and that he thought his letter was likely to be among the documents that Leo had got together when he came to deal with the 'social question'. He concluded by affirming that, as he did not know De Mun or his friends personally, he bore no animosity towards them as individuals.[11] When Rampolla replied on 31 July, he told Juring that he had shown his letter to Leo, together with Juring's pastoral letter and the pamphlet put out by de Pascal. The Pope had given considerable attention to Juring's argument, but it was a matter into which he was ill-prepared to enter, given its delicacy. Nevertheless, Leo strongly deplored the polemics in which some Catholics were engaging, and it was much better for them to refer their doubts and controversies to the Holy See for a solution. Meanwhile, instructions had been given to the Nuncio in Paris and Juring was advised, as Langenieux had been, to get in touch with him on the matter. What those instructions were, other than a plea for prudence and a cessation of public polemic, is not clear, but it is abundantly plain that the controversy continued to simmer both in Belgium and in France.[12]

Even in America, there was controversy, and Matthew Marshall, an economist, attacked Leo in the New York *Sun* on the grounds that he was like a man in the Sahara running after a mirage, especially when the condition of the working class in the Middle Ages was held up as a model. Marshall's specific criticism was probably justified, but it was unreasonable to single out one segment of the encyclical and condemn the whole as a result, especially when Leo had moved so far from the idea of renewing the old guild system of the Middle Ages.[13]

By 1892, the 'just wage' question had failed to become any clearer, but 65,000 German workers saw things in the best possible light and told Leo that they were in his debt for having said that workers should receive a wage 'ample enough to provide comfortably for themselves, their wives and their children'. They were also pleased that Leo had encouraged trade unions which meant that they had read the encyclical in the same favourable light as its authors had intended.[14] Nevertheless, a reaction to the encyclical had set in which was well illustrated in France, and especially, in the north of the country. In July 1894, Harmel was so concerned about the degree of opposition that he went down to Rome to see Rampolla. The Secretary of State was no passive defender of Leo, nor was he a mere cypher of Leo's thought. Indeed, it is clear that his role in the promulgation of *Rerum Novarum* was significant and, perhaps, decisive and it is not surprising that Harmel and others looked to Rampolla to secure papal approval for their activities and support for them in their moments of difficulty.

Harmel was well received by Rampolla and went back strengthened in his determination to stick by the encyclical. On his return, he wrote back to Rampolla and he included a draft of a letter he hoped that Leo would write to a Father Six, chaplain to the workers' movement in the north and editor of a paper, *Démocratie chrétienne*. Harmel wanted Leo to encourage Six and other priests, similarly disadvantaged because of their adherence to papal social teaching. Rampolla duly had the letter sent in Leo's name. It was firm, sensible and full of warmth and encouragement for *Démocratie chrétienne*. Leo also said that he hoped there would be genuine and willing collaboration between the clergy and the laity, and that there would be no discord on those questions which he had left open for further study. It ended with his blessing to all engaged in the same work as Six and encouraged them all to continue. Both Six and Harmel replied with gratitude.[15]

With his reply, Harmel included a copy of another letter which further illustrated the struggle between the old conservative element in the Church and the new vanguard of Christian democracy which had begun to take shape since 1891. This letter was written by a professor of philosophy, Father Bataille, to his Archbishop, Monsignor Tonnois of Cambrai. The Archbishop had recently forbidden priests who held teaching positions from writing in newspapers or reviews without his explicit permission. Bataille was writing to ask for that permission. He regarded it as his duty to communicate Leo's thoughts to the workers in particular as otherwise he would be obliged to stand back and watch 80,000 of them become revolutionary socialists while he did nothing. He promised to write based only on *Rerum Novarum* and the interpretation put on it by authority, in particular by the Congresses of Liège and Malines which had both been praised by Leo.

Tonnois replied to this humble and submissive request with a blunt refusal in which he said he had the full support of his archiepiscopal council.[16] It clearly meant that no priest, but, more especially, those priests capable of public writing by virtue of their knowledge and experience, could go into print, even in the form of an article, without submitting a request to the Archbishop. Were they permitted to do so, they had to submit their work to the censorship of the archdiocesan authorities. More importantly, it indicated that, in some areas in France, the very fact that a priest was prepared to stand publicly by Leo's teachings was likely to lead to repressive measures being taken against him. Bataille was a young priest, but he had started a workers' union with 1100 members and he had previously founded *Démocratie chrétienne* and more recently a workers' paper called *Le Peuple*. Such activities made his position powerful in public estimation, but also vulnerable in that he remained subject to ecclesiastical authority. Once forbidden to write, even in a paper which he had himself founded, Bataille was effectively silenced.

Another letter from Bataille also found its way into Rampolla's hands and probably also, through Rampolla, to Leo. It was written to Father Leon Montenis who lived in Rome and who must have taken it to the Secretary of State.[17] A note with it from Montenis to Rampolla suggested that Leo give an audience to Bataille. Rampolla wrote on it, 'Can he come to Rome?' There is no record of whether the audience took place. In his letter, Bataille said that, although he was bitterly disappointed at the refusal of Archbishop Tonnais to permit him to write publicly, he was not surprised at it. He was pained to see that his superior could ignore the main thrust of his request, the promulgation of papal teaching, and merely invoke an interdict on him. He related how both the Archbishop and Harmel had attended a Congress of Christian employers at Nouveaux in which an attack had been made upon the Belgian school of Christian sociologists. Harmel had defended it and accused the employers of northern France of being opposed to papal teachings.

Bataille then embarked upon an examination of the attitudes of the northerners by using a negative analysis. In order to prove that Leo's teachings were not accepted by the members of the 'retrograde' Church of the North of France, it was sufficient to put down their own beliefs in the form of propositions:

1. The situation of the workers is good, but in any case they deserve the greater part of the miseries they sometimes undergo.
2. A wage which is actually in force is always just.

3. Nothing should be done to raise wages.
4. Associations made up of workers are dangerous.
5. Professional unions, in which the workers are able to discuss with their employers such matters as hours of work, wages and conditions are useless, dangerous and utopian.
6. The only remedy to existing misery is the inculcation of morality amongst the workers and the creation of charitable organisations.

To Bataille it was clear that, if 'such gentlemen' wanted to prove that they were in agreement with the Pope on the 'social question', they had to accept a set of contrary propositions which he laid out as follows:

1. The greater part of the working class is in an unfortunate state and suffering unmerited misery.
2. Unions must be formed, at times made up of workers alone, at others of both workers and employers.
3. The question of wages and other similar questions ought by preference to be the province of workers' unions.
4. Even if a wage is agreed upon and is in conformity with existing laws it is not always a just wage.

Bataille told his Roman friend, 'There you have the declarations that the employers will never make.' Finally, he strongly held that the workers had an absolute right to a say in all the questions that affected their destiny and that they wanted to use that right while, at the same time, refusing to be duped by anyone. Probably Leo in Rome and Bataille in his humble parish in the North of France were unaware that they were laying down a strategy for Christian workers in a battle that was still at the stage of mere skirmishing. It would reach a fuller measure in the industrial countries of the world in the decades to come. The document known as *Rerum Novarum* was to remain the rallying cry of the Church on the 'social question' for the next century.

Nine

Conclusion

Many years ago, Bishop Basil Roper told me a story of an event in his life which he much regretted. Before the First World War he was a young priest at the cathedral presbytery in Ballarat, Australia. One day, he was called to the parlour where a young man awaited him with a small document in his hand. It was a copy of *Rerum Novarum* and the young man wanted the priest to explain its contents to him. The priest was forced to tell him that he could not do so because, although he was aware of Leo's encyclical, he was unable to explain it as he had never studied it. The young man went away unsatisfied and, according to the bishop, ceased from that day to interest himself in the social teachings of the Church to which he belonged. It was regrettable because he was James Scullin who later, in the very week of the Wall Street crash in New York in 1929, became the first Catholic prime minister of Australia.

Somewhat in the manner of James Scullin, I, too, wanted to know. I was already familiar with the text and meaning of *Rerum Novarum*, but I was not satisfied until I went further than that. I wanted to know why it was written. In the Vatican Secret Archives, the answer became clear. From all over the world, but especially from Europe, in French, Spanish, Portuguese, Italian, German, English, Latin, and in several other languages which I could not read, there were letters asking Leo to say something on the condition of the labouring masses. In the end, he responded, even if the work to which he put his name was not written by him, but every line became his as he watched over its creation.

But why was it important to know? Many people are familiar with the names of Alcide De Gaspari, Konrad Adenauer, Robert

130

Schuman, Carlo Sforza and Luigi Einaudi, to which countless others could be added. All of them were there at the making of the new Europe in the post-war period and all of them in their own way were the children of *Rerum Novarum*, as is still the case with those Christian Democrats who are leading the struggle for the rebirth of a united Europe today. To that degree Leo's encyclical is part of the history of modern Europe.

The influence of *Rerum Novarum* went further than those loyal sons of the Church who could be expected to accept its main teachings. At the time of its origins and birth in the 1880s and 1890s, the workers were being offered an alternative to capitalism in the form of socialism and eventually, after 1917, communism. Liberalism and other political systems that grew hand in hand with capitalism seemed to hold out little hope to the world of organised labour. Fascism became another alternative, but it soon revealed its inherent inhumanity. The fruits of *Rerum Novarum* as a rejection of fascism were seen in Italy in 1919 with the foundation of the Partito Popolare by the Sicilian priest, Luigi Sturzo, whose early years had been shaped by Leo's teachings. Under Mussolini, the Partito Popolare was stamped out with its members either intimidated, victimised or exiled. But on the ashes of fascism the Partito Popolare arose again in the form of the Christian Democrat Party, as happened also in Germany and France.

In some places there was another alternative and Australia saw the election of the first Labor government in the world when, for a few days in Queensland in 1899, a Labor Party was in office. Labor parties everywhere were constantly tempted by socialism and its tenets. But there were always those in the ranks prepared to proclaim, as Leo had done, that man was not the plaything of any economic or political system, and that the ultimate value was that of the human person whose dignity could never be impugned without enormous loss. Such parties often had a turbulent history as they tried to blend amalgams of radicals and conservatives, of those who wanted to overthrow capitalism and those who wanted to reform or 'civilise' it. In all of them, there was the determination not to be smothered in the embrace of sectaries, so that when Communist parties arose after 1917, based on the alleged uselessness of reformism, they did so outside the mainstream of political life.

Within the Catholic Church, *Rerum Novarum* was never forgotten. In fascist Italy, during the pontificate of Pius XI, there were attempts to revive the concept of a society based on corporations, and some made a connection between them and the encyclical *Quadragesimo Anno*, which Pius XI put out to commemorate the fortieth year of the publication of Leo's encyclical. For a time the corporations of the Fascist State had their day as a shameful mockery, but they bore no resemblance to the old guilds of the medieval period, nor to anything in the thinking of Vogelsang or the French experiments of the nineteenth century.

From Pius X (1903-14) through to John Paul II, encyclical after encyclical was issued which looked back to the principles enunciated by Leo, although they were successively developed much further and, especially by John XXIII and John Paul II. The simple statement of Leo in *Rerum Novarum* that no one may outrage with impunity that sacredness in man put there by God himself has been erected into the very *leit-motiv* of John Paul II.

It was never necessary for the Church to proclaim triumphantly that the regimes of Eastern Europe would collapse in on themselves, because from Leo's day it was held firmly that no society could endure of which man was not the centre. It is scarcely to be wondered at that John Paul II did not hesitate to give his prudent support to the Solidarity movement in Poland. A century ago, Leo XIII, in the pages of *Rerum Novarum*, had insisted on the right of the workers and argued cogently that any State which denied such a right, denied the basis of its own existence. Once that right had been conceded by the Polish authorities, it was inevitable that democracy would take shape, with the consequent collapse of the totalitarian State in Poland and elsewhere.

The tragedy of socialism is that, while theoretically based on the highest ideals of generosity, it has looked to force to shape the State and to mould individuals according to its ends. It could scarcely be expected that socialist leaders would have been familiar with the words of Leo. On the other hand, they might have done well to look into the heart of man where Leo's words were written by nature from the beginning of time. 'Man himself can never renounce his right to be treated according to his nature or to surrender himself to any form of slavery' and further, 'In this matter it is not a question of rights which a man is free to renounce, but of duties towards God which must be held as sacred.' It has not been merely a question of external threats or internal want that has brought socialism, in regime after regime, to its end. It has happened because millions of human beings finally refused to renounce their rights.

On the other hand, unrestrained capitalism has rarely been able to rise above an appeal to the worst in human nature, with greed so frequently the yardstick of its ethos. That is not to deny the evident benefit that has come to large sections of humanity through industrialisation and technological advances. The assertion or assumption that such progress is achievable only under unbridled capitalism is false. As a result, the task of every genuine labour movement has been, and is, to 'civilise' capitalism. The likelihood is increasingly clear that, in the reality of the world of today, 'civil society' in the democratic sense is possible only under a form of capitalism that is civilised and held in check by free institutions and by the rule of law. Without those reforms capitalism will continue to 'grind the faces of the poor' and in that eventuality some may turn to the task of christianising socialism. In any event, without Christianity, socialism has no future.

It was not for Leo or any pope after him to spell out a blueprint for society. His role was to set down the principles and leave the practical spelling out to others. If all he affirmed was that the human person is the creature of a benevolent Creator he would have said much. *Rerum Novarum* began with that as its first principle. It is for other ages, other men and women, to make it real in the world of their day.

It would be remiss of me to conclude without recognising the work of two men. One of them — Matteo Liberatore SJ — is named in these pages. Obscure and forgotten, his spirit lives on alongside that of Leo XIII in every page of *Rerum Novarum*. The other is Frederic Ozanam, founder of the St Vincent de Paul Society. Not only did his work push the Church into taking 'an option for the poor' but, years before it was written, he also believed in, and proclaimed, almost all that *Rerum Novarum* expressed.

Abbreviations

(C)   Latin translation of Liberatore's first Italian draft.
(L)   Liberatore's first Italian draft.
(L2)   Liberatore's second Italian draft.
PFA   Archives of Propaganda Fide.
(RN)   Official and final Latin version.
(Z)   Italian draft done by Cardinal Zigliara.
VSA   Vatican Secret Archives.

Notes

Chapter One

1. For the reaction of one part of the Catholic world, indeed its extremity, *see* John N. Molony, *The Roman Mould of the Australian Catholic Church*, Melbourne, 1969, ch. 3.
2. PFA. Vaughan to Cardinal Prefect, S.R., Anglia, 1878-1880, vol. 21, pp. 295-6. It was customary for bishops and priests from the English-speaking world to write to Rome in Latin or, if they knew it, Italian. Some American bishops wrote in French.
3. M.W. Gibson to Cardinal Prefect 12 December, 1878. ibid, p.297.
4. The best source for the life and pontificate of Leo is E. Soderini, *Il Pontificato di Leone XIII*, 2 vols. Milan, 1932. *See also* F. Hayward, *Léon XIII*, Paris, 1937.
5. Quoted in G. Antonazzi, (ed.) *L'Enciclica Rerum Novarum Testo Autentico E Redazioni Preparatorie dai Documenti Originali*, Rome, 1957, p.7.
6. Quoted in Jean-Yves Calvez SJ and Jacques Perrin SJ, *The Church and Social Justice: The Social Teachings of the Popes from Leo XIII to Pius XII (1878-1958)*, London, 1961, p.76.
7. *See* Angelo Brucculeri, SJ, *Il Giusto Salario*, Rome, 1938, and *Il Lavoro*, 4th ed. Rome, 1942. Brucculeri was writing during the Fascist period in Italy and wanted to see conformity between Catholic doctrine and Fascist practice, especially in relation to the corporate state. Nonetheless, he is clear and succinct on the historical background to the doctrinal propositions.
8. *See* Mario Cingolani, 'Padre Giocchino Ventura' in *Figure del Movimento Cristiano Sociale in Italia*, Turin, 1952, p.14.

9.   *See* Pietro Sinapoli di Giunta, *Il Cardinale Mariano Rampolla del Tindaro*, Rome, 1923.

10. Etienne Gilson, (ed.) *The Church Speaks to the Modern World: The Social Teachings of Leo XIII*. New York, 1954. pp. 188-199.

11. *ibid.*, pp. 29-54. Sandor Agócs, in his *The Troubled Origins of the Italian Catholic Labor Movement* 1879-1914, Wayne State University Press, Detroit, 1988, argues that, for Leo, Thomism was a particularly useful weapon to combat, 'perverse modern political and social doctrines' and that it was 'a return to the Middle Ages'. p.21 and p.20. While there may be some truth in this when viewed negatively, Leo was much more concerned that both theology and philosophy would have a solid basis and that any social doctrine which would flow from Thomism would be firmly established in the present, regardless of the past.

12. Greg Munro, *German Social Catholicism 1815-1914* University of Queensland, 1985, p.16.

13. *ibid*, pp. 17-18.

14. For De Gasperi, *see* Giulio Andreotti, *De Gasperi e il Suo Tempo Trento Vienna Roma*, 4th ed., Verona, 1974. pp. 24-91. During his long years of enforced silence in the Vatican Library, Alcide De Gasperi devoted a good deal of his spare time to preparing a book on the background to *Rerum Novarum* which was first published under the pseudonym Mario Zanatta, *I Tempi e gli Uomini che Prepararano La 'Rerum Novarum'* Milan, 1928. Other editions followed with the one which I have used being the third, published at Milan in 1945. De Gasperi's own background in the Trentino, his knowledge of French and German sources and his later involvement with the pioneers of Christian Democracy in Italy, notably Luigi Sturzo, made his book a reliable source which has been of considerable benefit to me. He deals with the three bishops on pp. 1-25 but he was unable to use the Vatican and Propaganda Archives which, for Leo's pontificate, were not

opened until *1979. The other, excellent source which I used was G. Munro, 'German Social Catholicism' where Ketteler is dealt with pp. 19-31. See also, Michael P. Fogarty, Christian Democracy in Western Europe 1820-1953*, London, 1957, pp. 164-5. See also, J. Joblin, 'Doctrine et Action sociale: reflexion sur l'evolution du mouvement social chretien avant et apres *Rerum Novarum'* in *Rerum Novarum Laborem Exercens 2000*, Rome, 1982, p.96.

15. See Ketteler from his *Freiheit, Autoritat und Kirche*, in G. Munro, 'German Social Catholicism', p.23.

16. A. De Gasperi, *I Tempi*, p.9.

17. For Mermillod see *ibid*, pp. 15-19.

18. For Manning see *ibid*, pp. 20-25 and E. S. Purcell, *Life of Cardinal Mannin, 2nd. ed., 2 Vols., London, 1896.*

19. Henry Manning, *A Pope on Capital And Labour: The Significance of the Encyclical Rerum Novarum*, London, 1933, pp. 21, 25, 31, 30, 36-7. Manning's article on the encyclical, therein reproduced, was first published in the *Dublin Review*, July, 1891.

20. PFA., S.R. 1885-86, vol. 26, Anglia, Manning to Cardinal Prefect p.664. Bagshawe had an unfortunate reputation for the flamboyant gesture and he went as far as to engage in public self-flagellation. His excesses aroused considerable opposition in his diocese. *See* letter of three senior priests of 8 May, 1879, in *ibid*, Vol. 21, pp. 89-104.

21. For the Liège Congress, *see* A. De Gasperi, *I Tempi*, pp. 83-105.

22. PFA, S.R. vol. 25, Bagshawe to Cardinal Prefect, 8 Sept., 1844; Manning to Cardinal Prefect, *ibid.*, 1883, p.572.

23. Virtue to Cardinal Prefect, 20 December, 1887, in *ibid.*, p.451.

24. Ullathorne to Cardinal Prefect, 1884, in *ibid., pp. 983-4.*

25. Rupert Graham to Leo XIII, 20 April, 1888 in *ibid.*, vol. 27, p.720. Turnerelli to Cardinal Simeoni, 20 February, 1888 in *ibid.*

26. Vaughan to Cardinal Prefect, 14 March 1887 in *ibid.*, pp. 107-8. Edmund Knight in *ibid.*, 1888, p.478.
27. O'Reilly to Cardinal Prefect, July 1879, in *ibid.*, vol. 21, p.556.

Chapter Two

1. A. De Gasperi, *I Tempi*, p.27. For an excellent article on De Gasperi's background see Mario Pendinelli, *'Al di la' degli "storici steccati."'* in *Il Messaggero*, Rome, 18 August, 1984, p.3.
2. *ibid.*, p.28. *See also* Michael P. Fogarty, *Christian Democracy*, p.430. By the 1880s, Mermillod, now cardinal, was chairman of the Union.
3. For Vogelsang *see* A. De Gasperi, *I Tempi*, pp. 30-46.
4. *ibid.*, p.39.
5. *ibid.*, p.46.
6. *ibid.*, p.40.
7. Jacob Burckhardt, *Judgements on History and Historians*, London, 1959, p.204.
8. *Quod Apostolici Muneris*. In: A. Keogh *The Pope and the People*, London, 1950, first published 1902, p.19.
9. *ibid.*, p.12.
10. *See* Michael P. Fogarty, *Christian Democracy*, pp. 189 and 251. Fogarty ranked Harmel with Cadbury and Seebohm Rowntree 'as one of the great pioneers of personnel management'. p.189. *See also* Jean-Yves Calvez SJ and Jacques Perrin SJ, *The Church*, p.404 and A. De Gasperi, *I Tempi*, pp. 69-71.
11. Maurice Maignen to de Mun quoted in *ibid.*, p.68.
12. For de Mun and La Tour du Pin *see* Jean-Yves Calvez and Jacques Perrin, *The Church*, pp. 404-6. De Mun was convinced that 'in this threefold concord of managerial responsibility, guild organisation and social legislation, we have a social system that will bring peace to the world of labour . . .' p.405.
13. *ibid.*, p.404.

14. *See* A. De Gasperi, *I Tempi*, pp. 83-86. The Liège Congress, with the contributions of Manning and Bagshawe on State intervention, has been touched on in Chapter 1. The question of the corporate State was not dealt with at Liège, but with the rejection of State control it was per se rejected also.

15. *See* John N. Molony, *The Emergence of Political Catholicism in Italy: Partito Popolare 1919-1926*, London, 1977, chapter 1.

16. Aquaderni to Jacobini, 24 November, 1881. In: VSA, *Epistolae ad Principes. Positiones et Minutae*, no 45, 2a *Littere riguardanti i Congressi cattolici e pellegrinaggi*, 1877-1887.

17. *ibid.*, the Lodi telegram is bound in with 150 others, many of the same ilk.

18. For the Catholic movement *see* Gabriele De Rosa, *Il Movimento Cattolico in Italia Dalla Restaurazione All'eta Giolittiana*, Bari, 2nd ed., 1972; F. Magri, *La Democrazia Cristiana in Italia*, 2 vols., Milan, 1954-5; see also Robyn Dutton, 'Opera dei Congressi' Ph.D. ANU, Canberra, 1990; A. De Gasperi, *I Tempi*, pp. 117-123.

19. *ibid.*, p. 118.

20. *ibid.*, p. 113.

21. *See* Federico Marconcini, 'Giuseppe Toniolo'. In: *Figure del Movimento Cristiano-Sociale in Italia*, Turin, 1952, pp. 53-55.

22. *See* A. De Gasperi, *ibid.*, pp. 127-8.

23. *ibid.*, pp. 131-2.

24. *ibid.*, pp. 133.

25. *ibid.*, pp. 134-58.

26. *ibid.*, pp. 138-9.

Chapter Three

1. A. Métin, *Le Socialisme sans Doctrine*, Paris, 1901. *From*: Frank Crowley, *A Documentary History of Australia:*

Colonial Australia 1875-1900 vol. 3, Melbourne 1980, p. 477

2. See the excellent article by Bede Nairn, 'George, Henry (1839-1897)' In: *Australian Dictionary of Biography*, vol. 4, 1851-1890, Melbourne, 1972, pp. 241-2. For George's partial but fleeting success in one country, Australia, see the article by F. Picard, 'Henry George and the Labor Split of 1891' in *Historical Studies*, no. 21, Melbourne, 1953, pp. 45-63.

3. *ibid.*, p.63.

4. For Roman material on the McGlynn case, *see* PFA, 1888, vol. 258, *ponente Cardinal Mazzella* pp. 1-30. *Also* Gerald P. Fogarty, *The Vatican and the American Hierarchy from 1870 to 1965*, Stuttgart, 1982 and Fogarty, *The Vatican and the Americanist Crisis: Denis J. O'Connell, American Agent in Rome. 1885-1903*, Rome, 1974.

5. PFA, 1888, vol. 258, pp. 3, 4, 10.

6. *ibid.*, p.7.

7. *ibid.*, p.4.

8. *ibid.*, p.6.

9 *See* Gerald P. Fogarty, *The Vatican*, pp. 87-91.

10. *ibid.*, p.103. Scholars are not permitted to consult the Archives of the Holy Office so that it is only from other correspondence that its workings are revealed.

11. McGlynn to Corrigan, 20 December 1886. The letter is in a Latin translation from the English original which is not in the Archives so my translation is back from the Latin. *See* PFA, vol. 384, 1888.

12. *ibid.*, Corrigan to Leo, 2 April, 1887.

13. The document contained fourteen pages and was written in French. Gibbons to Simeoni, 20 February, 1887. PFA. 1887, vol. 46, prot. 1265, pp. 295-310.

14. *ibid.*, prot. 968. pp. 357-8.

15. *ibid.*, Manning to Gibbons, 11 March, 1887. prot. 1113, p.447.

16. *ibid.*, vol. 258, 1888. The documentation on the case is voluminous.
17. *ibid.*, vol. 258, Barnes to Simeoni, 29 February, 1888.
18. *ibid.*, vol. 48, Lanier to Leo, 6 January 1888.
19. Lane, Hughes and Cotton are quoted in F. Picard, 'Henry George', pp. 47-8. In the opinion of Bede Nairn, with whom I agree, 'George's influence has been overrated by several historians and publicists'. *See* Bede Nairn, 'Henry George'. p.242.
20. T. Waddell, Croydon, Sydney, to Leo, no date, received 1 July 1890. PFA., S.R. Oceania 1890-2, vol. 17, pp. 184-5. Thomas Waddell, (1854-1940) was a very wealthy pastoralist and businessman who wrote extensively on public finance. He was a member of the Legislative Assembly and, briefly, Premier of New South Wales in 1904.
21. Joseph John Slavin to Propaganda, 3 May, 1890. *ibid.*, S.R. Anglia, vol. 28. p.750.
22. *See* E. Gilson, (ed.), *The Church Speaks*, p.278.
23. *See* Gerald P. Fogarty, *Denis J. O'Connell*, pp. 176-78 and Fogarty, *The Vatican*, pp. 101-2.
24. *ibid.*, p. 109.

Chapter Four

1. VSA., Segretaria Di Stato, 1891, Rubrica 1.
2. *ibid.* Epistolae ad Principes, Positiones et Minutae, 146 A and B.
3. Giovanni Antonazzi, (ed.) *L'Enciclica Rerum Novarum Testo Autentico E Redazioni Preparatorie dai Documenti Originali.* Prefazione di S.E.Mons. Domenico Tardini, Rome, 1957.
4. Tardini's notes in *Epistolae ad Principes*, VSA., 146 A.
5. *ibid.*
6. E. Soderini, *Il Pontificato di Leone XIII*, Milan, 1932, vol. 1, pp. 397-99.
7. Tardini's notes in *Epistolae ad Principes*, VSA, 146 A.

8. Tardini's notes in *Epistolae*, 146 A. Liberatore's text in a printed version is of 33 pages in a single column. Antonazzi divided it into 411 lines and it is to his version, which tallies exactly with the original, that I refer when quoting. Nevertheless, my examination of all the drafts and final text of the encyclical was based on the originals in the Volpini papers. I took note of the few but precious comments of Tardini and used Antonazzi where appropriate. To both, I acknowledge a general debt which in specific instances I detail in my footnotes.

9. Tardini's notes in *Epistolae, 146 A*.

10. *See* first page in *Epistolae, 146 A*.

11. Giovanni Antonazzi, *L'Enciclica*. p. 14 gives some examples.

12. The Latin word *opifex* means worker whether in industry or elsewhere and in its general sense means salaried worker as used in the encyclical. *See* Raimondo Spiazzi, OP (ed.) *I Documenti Sociali della Chiesa da Pio IX a Giovanni Paolo II (1864-1982)* Milan, 1983, p.93.

13. Giovanni Antonazzi, *L'Enciclica*, p.40, lines 1-6. Scriptural quotes were always given in Latin and Antonazzi noted that Liberatore slipped up slightly even in his very first quote. Liberatore had *'esurivi et dedistis mihi manducare . . . Nudus (eram) et cooperuistis me.'* The Vulgate reads *'esurivi enim, et dedistis mihi manducare . . .nudus, et cooperuistis me.'* (Matthew 25: 33, 36.)*ibid*, fn. 1. Liberatore clearly quoted from memory without recourse to a text, which reinforces my point about his haste to get the draft written.

14. *ibid*., (L), 10-11, p.39. The symbol (L) refers to Liberatore's first Italian draft, the numerals to the lines in Antonazzi.

15. *ibid*., (L) 17-18, 20-21, 24-5, p.39.

16. *ibid*., (L) 59-60, 70-71, pp. 40-41.

17. *ibid*., (L) 82-3, 85-7, p.41.

18. *ibid*., (L) 122-336, p.42.

19. *ibid*., (L) 137-9, p.42.

20. *ibid.*, (L) 149-50, p.43. Liberatore's words were '*ma abilitato a procacciarsi il vitto per sè e pe' suoi con moderato lavoro*'.

21. *ibid.*, (L) 165-8. p.43.

22. See *Civilta' Cattolica*, 19 February, 1890, s. XIV, vol. V, fasc. 953, pp. 558-61, and 5 March, 1890, s. XIV, Vol. V, fasc, 954, pp. 694-97.

23. Giovanni Antonazzi, *L'Enciclica*, (L) 159-69. p.43.

24. *ibid.*, fn. 164, p.43.

25. *ibid.*, (L) 170-96, pp. 43-4.

26. *ibid.*, (L) 197-8, p.44

27. Cappellazzi is quoted in Sandor Agócs, *The Troubled Origins*, p.61.

28. Giovanni Antonazzi, *L'Enciclica*, (L) The section on corporations runs from 197-252. That quoted is 242-4. p.45.

29. *ibid.*, (L) 239 and 242. p.45.

30. *ibid.*, (L) 257, p.46.

31. *ibid.*, (L) 283-90, pp. 46-7.

32. *ibid.*, (L) 300-309, p.47.

33. *ibid.*, (L) 310-22, p.47.

34. *ibid.*, (L) 325-6, p.47.

35. *ibid.*, (L) 326-33, pp. 47-8.

36. *ibid.*, (L) 333-83, pp. 48-9.

37. *ibid.*, (L) 384-411, pp.49-50. Liberatore, without naming it, was referring especially to Leo's encyclical, *Immortale Dei* of 1 November, 1885.

Chapter Five

1. As with Liberatore, I worked from Zigliara's printed text in the Vatican Archives, but used the line and pagination system that Monsignor Antonazzi so valuably provided.

2. Zigliara in Giovanni Antonazzi, *L'Enciclica*. (Z) 1-22, p.53. I will use the symbol Z for Zigliara's draft in all references.

3. *ibid.*, (Z) 51-3, 105-26, pp. 54-56.

4. *ibid.*, (Z) 150, 470-71, pp.56 and 64.

5. *ibid.*, (Z) 252-4, p.59.

6. *ibid.*, (Z) 871-887, 824-27, 805-7, pp. 74-5, 73.

7. *ibid.*, (Z) 790-4, 850-6, 255-65, 266, 710-11, 360-67, pp.72, 74, 59, 70, 62.

8. *ibid* (Z) 489-512, p.65.

9. *ibid.*, (Z) 514-81, 611-75, pp. 66-7, 68-9.

10. *ibid.*, (Z) 589-90, 894-905, pp.67, 75.

11. Volpini wrote his note on page 12 of the proofs of Zigliara's Italian text. Only a fragment remains of Volpini's Latin text which corresponds to lines 81-115 of Zilgiara's so that it is impossible to know whether Volpini made alterations to the text as he progressed and, especially, what he did with the words of Zigliara on birth control and the question of a just wage. See *ibid.*, p.15 and VSA, *Epistolae ad Principes, Positiones et Minutae* 146 A and B.

12. *See* first page of both manuscript and proof pages of the third draft in VSA for Volpini's note. Antonazzi came to the same conclusion that Liberatore was the principal agent in the third draft. *See ibid.*, pp. 17-19. Nonetheless, he used the symbol 'Z' when referring to the third draft, despite the fact that he acknowledged Liberatore as its principal author. To recognise that authorship I will use the symbol L2 when referring to it.

13. *ibid.*, (Z), 136-8, p. 56.

14. *ibid.*, (L2) 77-87, p.41; (Z) 136-8, p. 56; (L2) 395-421, p. 98. In Volpini's translation of L2 the 14 lines of Liberatore are omitted, p. 98.

15. *ibid.*, (L) 43-5, p.40.

16. *ibid.*, (L) 44-5, p. 40; (Z) 236-7, p. 59; (L) 306-9, p.47; (Z) 362-64, p.64; (L2) 1494-96, p. 152; (L) 149-50, p.43; (C) 1497-1502, p. 152; (C) 1523-28, p.152; (L2) 1494-96, p.152; *See also* Giovanni Antonazzi, *L'Enciclica*, pp. 20-21.

17. Marcellino Olaechea Loizaga, *Il Salario Justo*, Italian edition, Florence, 1954, pp. 29, 25.

18. *ibid.*, p. 19.

19. *See* John Rickard, *H.B. Higgins: The Rebel as Judge*, Sydney, 1984, pp. 171-5. The case was called the 'Harvester

judgement' because H.V. McKay built agricultural equipment and notably the McKay harvester.

Chapter Six

1. Volpini's words *'Ego plantavi 31 January 1891 ore 5 pom'* are found on the last page of the first manuscript draft of the Latin translation. The *'Ego plantavi'* is taken from Paul's words in I Corinthians 3: 6. 'I have planted, Apollo watered but God has given the increase.' Liberatore concluded his first and final drafts with those same words. Volpini did not use them in his translation, but mindful of them applied them to his own work. *See* texts in VSA *Epistolae ad Principes, Positiones et Minutae*, 146 A and B, and Giovanni Antonazzi, *L'Enciclica*. p.23, (L)411, p. 50, (L2) 2360, p. 192.

2. *ibid.*, (C) Title line p. 78 and 49, p. 80. I will use the symbol (C) for all references to Volpini's translation as Monsignor Antonazzi has done. It comes from the first word of his translation 'Caussa' p. 80.

3. Monsignor Antonazzi was determined to illustrate how difficult Volpini found his task by reproducing the four originals found in VSA in Volpini's handwriting in *ibid.*, Tav 8-11.

4. *ibid.*, (C) 100-124, p.82. The line numeration refers to the Italian text of (L2) and the Latin translation of Volpini (C).

5. *ibid* (C) 129-51, p.84.

6. *ibid.*, (C) 152-350, pp. 84-94.

7. *ibid.*, (C) 464-97, pp. 100-02.

8. *ibid.*, (C) 1175-1212, pp.134-6.

9. *ibid.*, (C) 1212-1223, p. 136.

10. *ibid.*, (C) 1320-34, p. 142. Curiously, none of the English translations of *Rerum Novarum* italicised the words 'with great reverence'. The official Italian translation did so however. The encyclicals of John Paul II are all based on the fundamental premise on human dignity as stated in

Rerum Novarum which is consistent with his own personalist concept of humanity.

11. *ibid.*, (C) 1335-54, pp. 142-4.
12. *ibid.*, (C)1433-35, pp. 148-55; (L) 300-16, p.47.
13. *ibid.*, (L2) and (C) 1486-1513, pp. 150-53. Volpini used collegium, as in the College of Cardinals, in his attempt to move from the concept of corporations. By such a usage, he did not take the step of excluding an association made up of employers and workers so that, on its own, collegium does not necessarily imply the concept of a trade union made up of workers alone.
14. *ibid.*, (L2) and (C) 1523-34, pp. 152-4.
15. *ibid.*, (C) 1528-32, pp. 152-4.
16. *ibid.*, (L2) and (C) 1540-54, p. 154. The Italian text had the word 'governi' instead of State and then went on 'which, because of their political ineptitude, are forced to render homage to the rich.' The latter words were omitted from the Latin text. From the Italian, 'democrazia', meaning the people or simply the plebs, the Latin became 'multitudo' and the word democracy was never used in the final text, here or elsewhere.
17. *ibid.*, (C) 1557-73, p. 154.
18. *ibid.*, (C) 1573-85, pp. 154-6.
19. *ibid.*, (C) 1610-12, p. 156.
20. Aquinas in his *Contra Impugnantes Dei Cultum et Religionem*, ch. 2, was quoted in *ibid.*, (C) 1646-7, p.158.
21. *ibid.*, (C) 1600-90, pp. 156-60.
22. *ibid.*, (L2) and (C) 2095-2105, p. 180.
23. *ibid.*, p.27 where the oral testimony of Monsignor Carlo Respighi is given. Respighi died in 1947 so he was able to pass his testimony directly to Tardini. There is no direct evidence that May Day was in mind for launching the encyclical but the Second International at Paris in 1889 had established May Day as the appropriate celebration for the world labour movement which was assuredly a fact not lost sight of in the Vatican. See William Z. Foster, *Outline*

History of the World Trade Union Movement, New York, 1956, p.142.

Chapter Seven

1. Monsignor Tardini and Antonazzi sought in vain for the rest of the text of Boccali in the Vatican Secret Archives and my search was equally in vain. Two of the three manuscript pages of Boccali are reproduced in Giovanni Antonazzi, *L'Enciclica*, as an appendix (unpaginated).

2. Boccali scratched out his first two attempts at the first part of the sentence so that the final version is difficult to read. Nonetheless, the general clarity of this handwriting was a relief after some of the previous manuscripts. *See* appendix in *ibid.*

3. The Latin text of the encyclical with its first words *Rerum Novarum* was published in *L'Osservatore Romano* on 19, 20, 21 May, 1891. For the Latin text, *see* Giovanni Antonazzi, *L'Enciclica*, pp. 79-197 in the last column.

4. *ibid.*, p. 205. See also *L'Osservatore Romano*, 23 May, 1891 for the authentic Italian version. It was not the same in some of its detail and wording as Boccali's version from which Volpini worked the final Latin. Who translated the Latin back to Italian for the authentic version is not known.

5. All subsequent English versions of the encyclical follow that first given in the London *Tablet* in 1891. Etienne Gilson, in his *The Church Speaks to the Modern World*, New York, 1954, p. 26 says that he compared the English translation with the original Latin. He saw no reason to change the first sentence. In this instance he might have done better to work also from the official Italian version and to have attempted seeing the Latin in its classical context.

6. *See* A. Freemantle, (ed.) *The Papal Encyclicals*, New York, 1956. p. 166.

7. *See* Giovanni Antonazzi, *L'Enciclica*, Boccali and Volpini, pp. 78-33, 7-11, 104-7, 124-7, 1597-8, pp. 79, 83, 157.

8. *ibid.*, Boccali and Volpini, 596-613, pp. 107-9.

9. *ibid.*, Boccali and Volpini, 2007-2361, pp. 177-193.

10. *ibid.*, pp. 30-33 and footnote 2 p. 21. Page proofs held in the VSA of the final version are fourfold, each with various additions, deletions and corrections. The first begins *'Excitata semel'* which was Volpini's first translation of Boccali's final Italian. The other three all begin with *'Rerum Novarum'*. Then there is the definitive text of 52 pages which has a white cover upon which Volpini wrote the date of 15 May 1891 with the words *'De Conditione Opificum Rerum Novarum'* after the date.

11. *ibid.*, footnote p. 197.

12. *ibid.*, pp. 18-19; *L'Osservatore Romano*, 17, 19, 20, 21, May, 1891; *La Civilta Cattolica*, s. XIV, vol. X, fasc. 938, 25 May 1891, pp. 513-47; *ibid.*, fasc. 984, June, 1891, pp. 641-75; *ibid.*, vol. XI, fasc. 985, 22 June, 1891, pp. 5-16.

13. See VSA, S. di Stato, 1891, fasc. 10. pp. 2627 and 2696, Gibbons to Leo XIII, Baltimore, 22 June, 1891.

14. Corrigan to Simeoni, New York, 16 June, 1891, APF, *Scritte Referite*, 1891, vol. 566, f. 654, p. 3260.

15. Charles Ward, Philadelphia, 26 May 1891, VSA, S. di Stato, R.I. fs. 13, p.88.

16. Henry George, *The Condition of Labour: An Open Letter to Pope Leo XIII*, Melbourne, 1930. First published 1891. VSA, Ireland to Rampolla, St Paul, 11 January 1894 fs. 12, p. 16316 The Vatican Secret Archives has a separate bundle entitled *'Enciclica Rerum Novarum de Conditione Opificum'* under which more correspondence is kept, including material until the late 1890s.

17. *ibid*, Bishop of Vannes to Leo, 6 June 1891, p. 2197.

18. *ibid.*, Place to Leo, 28 May, 1891; Rampolla to Place, 10 June, 1891, p. 2216.

19. *ibid.*, Spanish Ambassador to Leo, 6 June, 1891; Nuncio, Madrid, 8 June, 1891. A note in the Archives dated 8 June 1891 records the Polish translation. pp. 2209, 2240, 2261.

20. *ibid*., Guiseppe Toniolo to Leo, Padua, 15 June, 1891; Helleputte in Nuncio to Leo, Brussels, 13 June, 1891; document prepared by Association Catholique, France, June, 1891.
21. *ibid*., Nuncio to Leo, Munich, 5 June, 1981; Address from Catholic University, Lille, 29 June, 1981, Archbishop of Rheims to Leo, 6 July, 1891; Blum *et al* to Leo, 29 June, 1891; Bishop of Rodez and Vabres to Leo, 27 June, 1891. 2342, 2602, 2743, 2558, 2989.
22. Manning, Henry, *A Pope on Capital and Labour, the Significance of the encyclical Rerum Novarum*, London, 1933, pp. 3, 5, 7, 21, 23.
23. Herbert Vaughan to Leo, Salford, 30 July, 1891 in VSA, S.di S. 1891, R.I. fo. 11, p. 3011.
24. *ibid*., *See* telegram from Soc. Op. La Romanina to Leo, Rome, 1 June, 1891; Carnot to Leo, Paris, 31 May, 1891, fo. 13 telegram bundle and p.72.
25. *ibid*., Logue to Leo, 25 June, 1891, *ibid*., fo. 12, p. 3879.
26. PFA. *See* letter of state from John O'Mulley to Propaganda from Dublin, 10 September, 1888; letter unsigned, England, 10 May, 1888; letter of state from James MacVeagh, Dublin, 5 July, 1888. Because he had been ordained priest for 25 years, MacVeagh claimed that his opinion on the attitude of the Irish Catholic people to the pope had weight. S.R. Irelanda, 1888, vol., 43, fs. 265, 394, 482.
27. Moran to Kirby, Sydney, 29 June 1891. Irish College Archives, Rome; Kirby to Moran, 17 June, 1891. Sydney Archdiocesan Archives. I am indebted to Mr A.E. Cahill, History Department, Sydney University, for both references.
28. The printed circular, signed, 'Many Catholics' is found in PFA, S.R. Oceania, vol. 17, p.328 and registered on 29 November, 1890. *See ibid*., for Carr to Propaganda Fide, 12 July, 1891, p.780.
29. *Ballarat Star*, 14 April, 1893.

30. *See* PFA, S.R. Oceania, vol. 17, Frank O'Gorman to Propaganda Fide, 12 January, 1892.
31. Rogers to Leo XIII, Tapu Thamas, n.d., but probably late 1891, *In*: VSA, S.di Stato, 1891, R.I. fo. 12, p.37876.
32. Corrigan to Prop Fide, New York, 12 October, 1888; MacSweeney to Prop Fide, 29 July, 1888, PFA, S.R. Oceania, vol. 49, fs. 394 and 577. Father McGlynn died reconciled to the Church whose fundamental teachings he had never ceased to believe in.

Chapter Eight

1. Giovanni Antonazzi, *L'Enciclica*, RN. 1482-5. p.151.
2. *ibid.*, 1488-95, pp.151-3.
3. *ibid.*, 1523-28.
4. Goosens to Leo, Malines, 10 August 1891, in VSA, S. di Stato, S.R.I. fs. 11, p. 3219.
5. *ibid.*
6. Rampolla to Zigliara, Rome, 16 August, 1891, in *ibid.*, p.3219.
7. Rampolla to Goosens, 13 September 1891, in *ibid.*, p.3320.
8. Goosens to Rampolla, 13 September, 1891; Zigliara to Rampolla, 20 September, 1891; Rampolla to Goosens, 25 September, 1891; Goosens to Rampolla, 6 October, 1891; Rampolla to Goosens, 12 October, 1891, in *ibid*, pp. 3623, 3625, 3833.
9. *See* Giovanni Antonazzi, *L'Enciclica*. pp. 21-2.
10. Langenieux to Rampolla, 28 July, 1891; Rampolla to Langenieux, 1 August, 1891. VSA, S. di Stato, S.R. 1. fs, 11, p. 2938; A. De Gasperi, *I Tempi*, p. 133.
11. Juring to Rampolla, 21 July, 1891. *ibid.*, p. 2939. I could not find Juring's previous letter in the Archives.
12. *ibid.*, Rampolla to Juring, 31 July 1891.
13. *ibid.*, Monsignor Bernard O'Reilly to Rampolla, New York, 26 June 1891, in *ibid.*
14. *ibid.*, German Catholic Workers Societies to Leo. n.d. but reply sent 26 January, 1892, pp. 5386, 5452.

15. *ibid.*, Harmel to Rampolla, 24 July and 14 August, 1894; Six to Rampolla, 21 August, 1894 p. 19615.
16. Bataille to Tonnais, n.d. July, 1894. Tonnais to Bataille, 13 July 1894 in *ibid*.
17. *ibid.*, Bataille to Montenis, n.d. but probably early July 1894 as it was received at the Secretariat of State on 21 July, 1894.

Select Bibliography

Acta Leonis XIII. 26 vols. Rome, 1878-1903.

Acta Sanctae Sedis, vols. 11-25, Rome, 1878-1903.

Agócs, S., *The Troubled Origins of the Italian Catholic Labor Movement 1879-1914,* Milwaukee, 1988.

Andreotti, G. *De Gasperi e Il Suo tempo Trento Vienna Roma* 4th ed. Verona, 1974.

Antonazzi, G. ed. *L'Enciclica Rerum Novarum Testo Autentico e Redazioni Preparatorie Dai Documenti Originali,* Rome, 1957.

Are, G., *Economia e Politica Nell' Italia Liberale, 1890-1915,* Bologna, 1974.

Aubert, R; Fonzi, F; Passerin d'Entreves, E; Marrou, H.I; Vito, F. *Aspetti della Cultura Cattolica nell' età di Leone XIII.* Rome, 1961.

Aubert, R. *Lèon XIII* in *I Cattolici Italiani dall 800 ad Oggi,* Brescia, 1964.

Backstrom, P.N. *Christian Socialism and Co-operation in Victorian England: Edward Vansittart Neale and the Co-operative Movement,* London, 1974.

Bigo, P. *La Doctrine Sociale de L'Église,* Paris, 1966.

Brezzi, C. *Cristiani Sociali E Intransigenti, L'Opera di Medolago Albani Fino Alla 'Rerum Novarum'.* Rome, 1971.

Browne, H.J. *The Catholic Church and the Knights of Labor,* Washington D.C. 1949.

Brucelleri, A. *Il Giusto Salario,* Rome, 1938.

      Il Lavoro, 4th ed. Rome, 1942.

Byers, D. M. (ed). *Justice in the Marketplace: Collected Statements of the Vatican and US Catholic Bishops on Economic Policy, 1891-1984.* Washington, D.C. 1984.

Bynyon, G.C. *The Christian Socialist Movement in England.* London, 1931.

Calvez, Jean-Yves, 'Association et corporation chez les premiers commentateurs de *Rerum Novarum*' *Chronique Sociale de France,* December, 1957.

Calvez, Jean-Yves and Perrin, Jacques. *The Church and Social Justice: The Social Teachings of the Popes from Leo XIII to Pius XII (1878-1958),* London, 1961.

Camp, R. L. *The Papal Ideology of Social Reform: A Study in Historical Development 1878-1967.* Leiden, 1969.

Candeloro, G. *Il Movimento Cattolico in Italia.* Rome, 1953.

Carlen, M.C. *Dictionary of Papal Pronouncements: Leo XIII to Pius XII (1873-1957),* New York, 1958.

The Papal Encyclicals, 5. vols. Wilmington, N.C. 1981.

Cavallera, F. *Précis de la Doctrine Sociale Catholique,* Paris, 1931.

Chenu, M.D. *La 'Doctrine Sociale' de L' Église Comme Ideologie.* Paris, 1979.

Cingolani, M. 'Padre Giocchino Ventura' in *Figure del Movimento Cristiano Sociale in Italia,* Turin, 1952.

Curran, C.E., McCormick, Richard A. SJ (eds). *Official Catholic Social Teaching: Readings in Moral Theology, No.5.* New York, 1986.

Defourni, E. *Les Congrès Catholiques en Belgique.* Louvain, 1908.

De Gasperi, Alcide. *I Tempi e Gli Uomini Che Prepararano La 'Rerum Novarum'.* First published under the pseudonym, Mario Zanatta, Milan, 1928. This edition Milan, 1945.

De Rosa, G. *Il Movimento Cattolico in Italia Dalla Restaurazione All Eta Giolittiana,* Bari, 2nd. ed. 1972.

Desrochers, J. *The Social Teaching of the Church.* Bangalore, 1982.

Dorr, D. *Option for the Poor: A Hundred Years of Vatican Social Teaching.* New York, 1983.

Duroselle, J.B. *Les Débuts du Catholicisme Social en France (1822-1870).* Paris, 1951.

Ellis, J.T. *Cardinal Gibbons.* 2 vols. Milwaukee, 1952.

Fogarty, G.P. *The Vatican and the Americanist Crisis: Denis J. O'Connell, American Agent in Rome, 1885-1903.* Rome 1975.

    The Vatican and the American Hierarchy from 1870 to 1965. Stuttgart, 1982.

Fogarty, M.P. *Christian Democracy in Western Europe 1820-1953. London, 1957.*

Foster, W.Z. *Outline History of the World Trade Union Movement.* New York, 1956.

Fremantle, A. *The Papal Encyclicals in their Historical Context,* New York, 1956.

Gambasin, A. *Il Movimento Sociale Nell' Opera dei Congressi, 1874-1904.* Rome, 1958.

George, H. *The Condition of Labour; an Open Letter to Pope Leo XIII.* Melbourne 1930. First published 1891.

de Gerard, E. *Ketteler et la Question Ouvrière.* Berne, 1896.

Gerin, P. *Catholiques Liégeois et la Question Sociale (1883-1914).* Brussels, 1959.

Gibbons, E. (ed.). *Seven Great Encyclicals.* New York, 1963.

Gilson, E. (ed). *The Church Speaks to the Modern World: The Social Teachings of Leo XIII.* New York, 1954.

Giordani, I. (ed.) *Le Encicliche Sociali dei Papi da Pio IX a Pio XII, 1864-1956.* Rome, 1956.

Goyau, G. *Ketteler,* Paris, 1908.

Hayles, E.E.Y. *The Catholic Church in the Modern World: A Journey from the French Revolution to the Present,* New York, 1960.

Hayward, F. *Léon XIII.* Paris, 1937.

Henroit, P.J.; DeBerri, E.P.; Schultheis, M.J. *Catholic Social Teaching: Our Best Kept Secret*. Revised and enlarged ed. New York, 1988.

Hogan W. *The Development of Bishop Wilhelm Emmanuel von Ketteler's Interpretation of the Social Problem*, Washington, D.C., 1946.

Hoog, G. *Histoire du Catholicisme Social en France*. Paris, 1946.

Husslein, J. *The Christian Social Manifesto; An Interpretative Study of the Encyclicals Rerum Novarum and Quadragesimo Anno*. Milwaukee, 1939.

Social Wellsprings: Fourteen Epochal Documents by Pope Leo XIII. Milwaukee, 1940.

Jarlot, G. Historia Documentorum Ecclesiae de Re Sociali a Leone XIII ad Pium XII. Rome, 1955-56.

Les avants-projects de 'Rerum novarum' et les 'Anciennes Corporations' in *Nouvelle Revue Theologique*, LXXXI, 1959.

'L'encyclique "Rerum Novarum" devant le problème du juste salaire.' in *La Vie Economique et Sociale*. XXXII, 1959.

Doctrine Pontificale et Histoire: L'Enseignement Social de Léon XIII, Pie X et Bendit XV Vu Dans Son Ambiance Historique (1878-1922) Rome, 1964.

Joblin, J. *Doctrine et Action Sociale: Reflexion Sur L'Evolution du Movement Social Chretien, Avant et Apres Rerum Novarum* in *Rerum Novarum Laborem Exercens 2000*, Rome, 1982, ps. 89-113.

Jostock, P. *Der Deutsche Katholizismus und Die Uberwindung des Kapitalismus*. Regensburg. 1932.

Keogh A. *The Pope and the People; Select Letters and Addresses on Social Questions*. 1st ed. London, 1902, This ed. London, 1950.

Kothen, R. *La Pensée et L'Action Sociale des Catholiques (1789-1944)* Louvain, 1945.

L'Enseignement Social de L'Église. Louvain, 1949.

Kissling, J.B. *Geschichte der Kulturkampf im Deutschen Reiche.* Fribourg, 1911-16.

Leslie, S. *Henry Edward Manning: His Life and Letters.* London, 1921.

Levanuet, R.P. *La Vie de L' Église sous Léon XIII.* Paris, 1930.

Liberatore, M. *Principi di economia politica.* Rome. 1889.

Loizaga, M.O. *Il Salario Justo.* Italian ed. Florence, 1954.

de Lubac, H. *Catholicisme, les Aspects Sociaux du Dogme.* Paris, 1930.

Lutz, H. *I Cattolici Tedeschi Dall' Impero Alla Repubblica.* Brescia, 1970.

MacLaren, D. *Private Property and the Natural Law.* Oxford, 1948.

Magri, F. *La Democrazia Cristiana in Italia.* 2 vols. Milan, 1954-55.

Mangano, V. *Il Pensiero Sociale e politico di Leone XIII,* Milan, 1913.

Manning, H. *A Pope on Capital and Labour: The Significance of the Encyclical 'Rerum Novarum',* London, 1933.

Marconcini, F. 'L'unità del pensiero economico di Giocchino Pecci negli scritti anteriori e posteriori alla "Rerum novarum".' In: *Il XL Anniversario Della Enciclica 'Rerum Novarum'* Milan, 1931.

'Guiseppe Toniolo' in *Figure del Movimento Cristiano-sociale in Italia.* Turin, 1952.

Masse, B.L. *Justice for All: An Introduction to the Social Teachings of the Catholic Church.* Milwaukee, 1964.

Mattai, G. *Il Lavoro: Le Encicliche Sociali; Dalla 'Rerum Novarum' alla 'Laborem Exercens'.* Padua, 1982.

Mollette, G. *Albert de Mun,* Paris, 1970.

Molony, J.N. (ed.) *Towards a New Age of the Human Person*, Melbourne, 1963.

The Emergence of Political Catholicism in Italy: Partito Popolare 1919-1926. London, 1977.

Munro, G. 'German Social Catholicism 1815-1914' University of Queensland, 1985.

Nairn, B. 'George, Henry (1839-1897) in *Australian Dictionary of Biography*. vol. 4. 1851-1890.

Picard, F. 'Henry George and the Labor Split of 1891' in *Historical Studies*. no. 21. Melbourne, 1953.

Poynter, J.W. *The Popes and Social Problems*, London, 1949.

Purcell, E.S. *Life of Cardinal Manning*. 2 vols. 2nd. ed. London, 1896.

Rerum Novarum Laborem Exercens 2000 Symposium Rome, 1982.

Rezsohazy, R. *Origines et Formation du Catholicisme Social en Belgique*. Louvain, 1958.

Rickaby, J. 'A Commentary on the Encyclical Letter of May 15 1891, *On the Condition of the Working Classes*' in *The Month*, 91, 1898.

Rickard, J. *H.B. Higgins: The Rebel as Judge*. Sydney, 1984.

Riposati, B. 'La preparazione della "Rerum novarum" (dai documenti originali dell' Archivio segreto vaticano.' In: *Vita e Pensiero*, XL, 1957.

Ritter, E. *Die Katholisch-Soziale Beweguns Deutschlands im 19 Jahrhundert und der Volksverein*. Cologne, 1954. Italian translation, *Il Movimento Cattolico-Sociale in Germania nel XIX Secolo e Il volksverein*. Rome, 1967.

Riva Sanserverino, L. *Il Movimento Sindicale Cristiano dal 1850 al 1939*, Rome, 1950.

Rollet, H. *L'Action Sociale des Catholiques en France (1871-1901)*. Paris, 1947.

Romani, M. 'La preparazione della "Rerum novarum".' In: *Vita e Pensiero*, XLIV, 1961.

Rossini, G. (ed.). *Aspetti Della Cultura Cattolica Nell' età di Leone XIII*. Rome, 1961.

Rovan, J. *Le Catholicisme Politique en Allemagne*. Paris, 1956.

Sangnier, M. *A. De Mun*. Paris, 1932.

Schillebeeckx, E. *'Portée théologique du magistère en matière sociale et politique'*. *Concilium*, XXXVI. 1968.

Scoppola, P. *La Democrazia nel Pensiero Cattolico del Novecento*. Turin, 1972.

Secco Suardo, D. *Da Leone XIII A Pio X*, Rome, 1958.

Sholl, S.C. 150 *Anni di Movimento Operaio Cattolico nell' Europa Centro Occidentale (1789-1939)*. Padua, 1962.

Sinapoli di Giunta, P. *Il Cardinale Mariano Rampolla Del Tindaro*. Rome, 1923.

Soderini, E. *Il Pontificato di Leone XIII*. 2 vols. Milan 1932.

'Per la genesi della "Rerum Novarum"' in *Nuova Antologia,* Rome, 16 May, 1916.

Spadolini, G. *L'Opposizione Cattolica da Porta Pia al '98*. Florence, 3rd ed. 1955.

Spiazzi, R. (ed.). *I Documenti Sociali Della Chiesa da Pio IX a Giovanni Paolo II (1864-1982)*. Milan, 1983.

Sturzo, L. *Church and State*, 2 vols. Notre Dame, 1962.

Talmy, R. *Aux Sources de Catholicisme Social: L'École de la Tour Du Pin*. Paris, 1963.

Tanghetti, F. *La Questione Sociale Nel Pensiero di S. Tommaso e Il Suo Influsso Nelle Encicliche Sociali*. Rome, 1977.

Troeltsch, E. *The Social Doctrines of Churches and Christian Groups*, New York, 1960.

de T'Serclaes, C. *Le Pape Léon XIII: Sa Vie, Son Action Religieuse, Politique et Sociale*. 3 vols. Lille, 1895-1906.

Vilder, A.R. *A Century of Social Catholicism*, 1820-1920. London, 1964.

Wallace, L.P. *Leo XIII and the rise of Socialism*. Durham, N.C. 1966.

Watt, L. *Catholic Social Principles: A Commentary on the Papal Encyclical 'Rerum Novarum'*. London, 1929.

Weiss, C.F. 'Corporatism and the Italian Catholic Movement' University of Yale. 1955.

Wynne, J.J. *The Great Encyclicals of Pope Leo XIII*, New York, 1903.

Zaninelli, S. *'Dalla "Rerum novarum" ai messaggi di Giovanni XXIII: Linee di interpretazione del pensiero sociale della Chiesa.'* In: Vita e Pensiero, XLIV, 1961.

Part II

Rerum Novarum

The following translation is based on the official Latin version of *Rerum Novarum*, and the authentic Italian version published in *L'Osservatore Romano*. I have not hesitated to use some phrases from the earliest English version of 1891, given the felicity of expression which it often had. I had decided to use a modern translation of the Scriptures for passages taken from the Bible, but when I discovered that the time-honoured *Increase and multiply* from Genesis was rendered as *Have many children*, I instantly changed my mind. In order to make the text complete, I have included, within brackets, three quotations from Scripture and one from Thomas Aquinas, which the encyclical had as footnotes. Although the encyclical had no section headings, I have inserted my own to facilitate the reading of the text.

The Worker Question

The burning desire for change, which for so long has begun to stir up the masses, inevitably had to make its presence felt in the related field of economics as well as in politics. A combination of factors, together with a decline in moral standards, has given rise to conflict. Those factors are the prodigious progress in science and in industry; the changed relations between employers and workers; the accumulation of riches in the hands of a few; the everspreading presence of poverty; the feeling of its own power that is developing among the more vital elements of the working class and the strong bonds they have forged among themselves.

Worker question of gravest importance

Today, the situation is so serious that it fills many minds with fearful apprehension, it consumes the talents of the learned, the meetings of the wise, the assemblies of the people, the deliberations of legislators and the councils of rulers. Indeed, there is no other question of greater moment in the world today. In the past Venerable Brothers, for the good of the Church and society, we have written to you on several occasions. It was timely to do so in order to refute false opinions by dealing with such matters as political power, human liberty, the Christian constitution of the State, and other similar matters. Today, we believe that, for the same reason, we must treat of the worker question. We have touched upon it when necessary on more than one occasion, but conscious of our Apostolic office, we are moved in this letter to deal with it directly and fully, in order to highlight the principles of truth and justice upon which the question will be resolved.

A difficult question

This whole matter is not easily dealt with and it is not without
its dangers. It is hard to define the precise relations between
owners and workers, between capital and labour. There is
danger in it because, day-by-day, wily and restless men take
advantage of the state of confusion which exists to cloud
judgement and agitate the masses. Whatever the case, it is clear,
and there is general agreement on this, that it is necessary to
come forward with appropriate remedies so as to help the
workers, most of whom find themselves, through no fault of their
own, reduced to a miserable condition.

Reasons for the sufferings of the workers

The workers' guilds were abolished in the last century without
anything being put in their place, at precisely the same time as
public institutions and legal systems were being dechristianised.
Thus, it has come to pass that, little by little, the workers have
been abandoned and left without any defence. They find
themselves at the mercy of greedy employers and a system of
unrestrained competition.

To this situation must be added the evil of rapacious usury
which, although condemned so often by the Church, nonetheless,
with like injustice, is still practised by covetous and grasping
men under other forms. Meanwhile, a monopoly of production
and commerce has fallen into the hands of a small number of
tycoons who have laid upon the teeming masses of the labouring
poor a yoke little better than that imposed by slavery itself.

The socialist solution is harmful and unjust

To remedy these disorders, the socialists, stirring up hatred of
the rich among the poor, hold that it is necessary to abolish the
private possession of goods, and replace it with a common form
of ownership under the control of local or national governments.
By this transformation of private into collective property, and
with the provision to every citizen of equal access to public

utilities, the socialists believe that the present evil state of things will be set aright. But such a way of acting, rather than removing the sources of conflict, would do no other than harm the workers themselves. Moreover, it would be unjust because it would set aside the rights of legitimate owners, change radically the functions of the State and throw the whole community into disorder.

The right to private property

It is assuredly not hard to understand that the acquisition of private property is the reason which motivates the worker when he engages in his labours. If he uses his strength and skill to the advantage of another he does so in order to obtain the necessities of life for himself. He therefore acquires a true and perfect right, not only to his wages, but also to use them as he sees fit. It follows that, if he lives sparingly, saves for his future security and then invests his savings in a piece of land, that land is simply his wages under another form. Consequently, it becomes his own property exactly as his wages were. It is clear to everyone that ownership consists in this kind of power over property of whatever kind. By transferring into public ownership all forms of private ownership, the socialists thereby take from the worker the freedom to dispose of his wages as he sees fit, and rob him of the right and the hope of bettering his domestic condition and his own personal state in life. Such a way of acting would make the existence of the workers even more unhappy than it is at present.

What is even worse, however, is the fact that the remedy put forward by the socialists is a clear injustice because private property is held by a right which stems from the nature of man. In this whole matter there is a wide difference between a man and an animal. An animal has no control over itself except through the use of its instinctive desires to preserve its own life and to propagate its own kind. Those instincts keep it alert and active, but they also determine and circumscribe everything done by the animal. Both these instincts can be satisfied by the use of means which an animal has within its range, and it is unable to act otherwise because it is motivated only by its senses.

Man is not a mere animal

The nature of man is totally different. He possesses animal life in its fullest, so that he also can use and enjoy material goods like other animals. But his animal life does not restrict man's human nature because it is greatly inferior to it and is subject to it. The great privilege of the human person, which is fundamental to his being and which distinguishes him from brute creation, is to be able to use his intelligence or, more exactly, his power of reason. Precisely because he has this power, a man must be granted more than the mere use of those material things which are common to the animal kingdom. He must also have the right to possess them as stable property, not only in the form of things which are consumed by their use, but also those that remain for further use in the future.

All this becomes clearer the more man's nature is contemplated. His consciousness embraces the future as well as the present and his freedom is such that he is master of his own destiny, guided by the eternal law and universal providence of God. He ought, therefore, to be able to select the means which he judges appropriate for the maintenance of his own life, not only for a passing moment, but also for the future. Because the needs of man rotate, in the sense that what he needs today he will also need tomorrow, it is fitting that nature has given to him the right to stable and permanent possessions, proportionate to his recurring needs. That kind of stability is to be found only in the earth and its fruits.

Mother earth

There is no need to turn to the State in this matter because man precedes the State and, before the foundation of any State, he already had from nature the right to provide for himself. The fact that God gave the earth for the use and enjoyment of the whole human race is not in conflict with the right to private property. That gift of the earth was not meant as a kind of common and indiscriminate form of property. Nevertheless, no part of it was given to anyone in particular, but it was left to the industry of man and the special laws of individual nations to determine the manner in which it would be divided up. Although the earth is apportioned out amongst individual owners, it remains at the service and for the benefit of all because everyone receives their sustenance from it. Those who do not own land do their part by their labour, so that it may be rightly said that the universal means of providing for life is work done in cultivating one's own land, or by using one's gifts in work of other kinds. Such work is paid for, ultimately, by the many fruits of the earth, or by that which is exchanged for the produce of the earth.

This is another proof that the right to private property is in agreement with the law of nature. Truly, the earth provides in abundance all that is needed to maintain and perfect human life, but only to the degree that man cultivates it and expends his care on it. When man uses his mind and body to obtain the goods of the earth, he thereby joins to himself that portion of nature's field which he cultivates. In so doing, he leaves an imprint of his own personality upon it, so that he is justly able to claim it as his own, and demand from others respect for his ownership.

Rejection of outmoded theories

The reasons as stated above are so evident that it is difficult to understand how they can be contradicted by those who wish to give life again to contradictory and utopian theories. They concede to man the use of the earth and its various fruits, but claim that he has no right of ownership to the soil on which he has built or to the field that he has cultivated. Cannot such people realise that in such a way they bid fair to defraud man of the effects of his work? The field he has ploughed and cultivated with skill is not what it was before, because it has been transformed from a wilderness into earth which bears fruits; it was barren but now it flourishes. That improvement takes shape in such close conformity to the land itself that it becomes part of it. What kind of justice would it be were another, who has not cultivated that soil, to come in and enjoy its fruits? As an effect follows a cause, so also the fruits of work should belong to him who does the work.

Divine and natural laws authorise right to private property

Therefore, with good reason, the human race has paid little heed to extreme theories, but, with an eye only to the law of nature, has found in that law itself the foundation of the division of property. Consequently, the right to private property has been recognised as pre-eminently in conformity with human nature and conducive to social harmony, so that it has been solemnly authorised throughout the ages. Civil laws also, to the extent that they are just, derive their authority and power to bind from the same law and they too conform and enforce the same right. The seal of the divine law also authorises that right and goes as far as to forbid, in severe terms, even the desire to possess that which belongs to another. *Thou shalt not covet they neighbour's wife; nor his house, nor his field, nor his man-servant, nor his maid-servant, nor his ox, nor his ass, nor anything that is his.* (Deut.: 21).

The family and its rights

This right to private property increases in value when it is considered in relation to social and domestic society. In choosing his state in life a man is certainly free. He can either follow the evangelical counsel of virginity, or bind himself in matrimony. The right to marry is both natural and primal and no human law can abolish it, nor limit in any way the scope ordained by God for it when He said, *'Increase and multiply'* (Gen. 1: 28). The use of the right to marry gives rise to the family, which is certainly a small society but, nonetheless, a true one. It is older in its origins than any State and, as a result, it has rights and obligations independent of any State.

It follows that what we have said about the right to property in respect of the individual person must be applied to a man as head of a family. In fact, such a right is more weighty the more the family is extended. The maintenance of his children falls upon the father by a most holy law of nature. Likewise, it is natural for the father to want to provide his children with all they need so that they may be decently freed from want throughout the difficult course of their lives. He does this because his children are the fruit of his paternity and, in a special way, give life to his own personality. The fact remains that he cannot provide adequately for his children unless through the ownership of productive property which, by inheritance, he can pass on to them.

As we have said, the family, as well as the State, is also a true society which is ruled by its own paternal authority. On that account, provided the limits determined by its purpose are observed, the family has rights which are at least equal to those of civil society in the choice and use of means necessary for its preservation and legitimate independence. We say at least equal rights because, as the domestic household is logically and historically antecedent to civil society, its rights and duties are also antecedent and more firmly founded in nature. If a citizen or a family entered civil society and found that the State, instead of giving help, placed obstacles in the way of their well-being and diminished, rather than safeguarded, their rights, such a society would be one to flee from, rather than embrace.

Duty of the State towards the family

It is a great and pernicious error, therefore, to propose that the State can interfere at will in the sanctuary of the family. It is certainly the case that, if a family, lacking the help of friends, were to find itself in grave distress from which it could not emerge by its own efforts, it is proper that public authority should intervene, given that each family is part of civil society. Likewise, in the case of a household in which there has been a grave violation of mutual rights, public authority should intervene to force each party to render to each other their proper due. This is not to usurp the rights of the citizens, but to secure and safeguard them. There, however, the State must stop, because, to go further, is to exceed the bounds of nature. The authority of the father is such that it can neither be extinguished nor absorbed by the State because it has the same source as life itself. *The child forms a part of the father* and is in a sense the amplification of his own personality. Strictly speaking, therefore, the child does not enter into and participate in civil society except through the family into which it is born. For the very reason that the children form *naturally a part of the father . . . they are under the care of their parents before they attain the use of free will* (Thomas Aquinas, Summa Theol., 2a-2ae, Q. x. art. 12). Hence, the Socialists, by substituting for the care of children by the parents, that of the State, act *against natural justice* and destroy the structure of the home.

Harmful effects of denial of right to private property

As well as being an injustice, the abolition of the right to private property would clearly cause confusion and disorder amongst all sections of the community, accompanied by the subjection of the citizens to a cruel and hateful bondage. The way would be open to envy, to recrimination and to discord; the very sources of wealth would necessarily dry up because all incentive would be removed from the use of individual talent and industrious activity, and the dreamed-of equality would only be a universal condition of misery and degradation. It is, therefore, necessary to conclude that the main teaching of socialism on the need for a communal possession of goods must be thoroughly rejected because it is injurious to those whom it proposes to help, it is repugnant to the natural rights of individuals, it upsets the proper structure of the State and disturbs common peace. When it comes to taking action to better the condition of the working masses, there can be no other principle to base such action on than standing firm on the right to private property. With that as our starting point, we shall now explain how to find the required remedy to the worker question.

Need of Church and religion to help solve worker question

We proceed with confidence and with right on our side because the problem is such that no solution can be found without turning to religion and to the Church. Since it is our duty to be the guardian of religion and to use the means that are at the disposal of the Church, we would seem to betray our office were we to remain silent. Certainly, the solution to such a difficult problem also requires the work and effective co-operation of others. We mean the rulers of States, employers and the wealthy, and indeed the workers themselves, for whom we are making this plea.

Nonetheless, we say without hesitation that all the future striving of men in this matter will be aimless if the Church itself is marginalised. In fact, it is the Church that draws teachings from the Gospels which can help to resolve present conflicts or at least make them less bitter. By its teachings, the Church not only opens and instructs minds, but also moulds the lives and habits of individuals; the Church, with its wide range of organisations, helps to improve the condition of the workers; the Church wants, and indeed longs for, all social classes to use their wisdom and strength to work together in harmony so that they may foster the interests of the workers in the best possible way. Finally, the Church believes that, within defined limits, the very laws and authority of the State should be used to this end.

Reality must be faced

The first thing to remember is that we must face reality about the human condition, and that it is, therefore, impossible to reduce everyone to the same level. The Socialists assuredly agitate to that end, but anything that is contrary to human nature will fail. Amongst men, there are naturally many and great differences; all do not possess the same intelligence, skill, health or strength and from these inevitable differences, different situations in life follow.

The result is to the advantage both of the individual and of society itself, because every community needs differing aptitudes and gifts and the principal impulse which moves individuals to act stems from their own personal situation in life. Insofar as manual labour is concerned, a man in the very *state of innocence* itself would not have remained idle. The things he would have freely done in that state for his own happiness became necessary after his fall so that he might painfully make up for his disobedience; *Cursed be the earth in thy work; in thy labour thou shalt eat of it all the days of thy life (Gen. 3: 17).*

In like manner, sorrow will never be absent from the world because the due consequences of sin are bitter, harsh and difficult to bear and they will accompany man to the tomb. It is, therefore, the lot of humanity to suffer and endure. Strive as much as he likes, no force or artful dodge will ever succeed in banishing human suffering. Those who say they can achieve this, and who hold out to sorrowing humanity a promise of a life free of pain and trouble, full of peace and enjoyment, delude the people and lead them on a path which will result in even worse evils than the present ones. The best thing to do is to accept the reality of the human situation and to look elsewhere, as we have said, for a remedy to its woes.

Rejection of inevitability of class conflict

The worst evil in the present situation is to accept the idea that one class is spontaneously the enemy of the other class, so that the wealthy and the workers are inevitably intended by nature to be locked in conflict. Such a concept is so contrary to reason and truth that it flies in the face of reality. Just as in the human body, the various members work together and combine into a harmonious symmetry, so also nature intends the two classes to work together in society and create a precious equilibrium. Each class has an absolute need of the other; there can be no capital without labour, nor labour without capital. Beauty and good order are the results of mutual agreement, whereas perpetual conflict can only result in confusion and barbarism.

How to eliminate conflict

Now, in order to bring peace out of conflict, and to eliminate the roots of conflict, the power of Christian institutions is extraordinary and everywhere apparent. First of all, the teachings of Christianity, of which the Church is both interpreter and guardian, are a powerful means of reconciling and bringing together the wealthy and the workers by reminding both of their mutual duties, starting with those that are imposed by justice. The obligations of justice, insofar as white- and blue-collar workers are concerned, are the following: fully and loyally to perform the work that has been freely and justly agreed to; not to damage the property nor offend the person of the employer and not to engage in acts of violence or mutiny in the defence of their own rights. Finally, they must avoid getting involved with men of bad faith, who promise great things which so often result in useless regrets for the past and in the ruination of future prospects.

Duties of capitalists and employers

The capitalists and the employers have the following duties: not to treat their workers as slaves, but to respect the equality of their personal human dignity which is rendered noble by its Christian character. It is not work that degrades man. In the light of reason and with the eye of faith, it is clear that work ennobles man because, through it, he can earn an honourable livelihood. That which is truly shameful and inhuman is to use men as if they were mere objects of gain, and force them to work beyond their physical and mental powers. Likewise, it is necessary to keep in mind religion and the good of his soul when dealing with the worker. The employer is bound to see that the worker has a convenient opportunity to exercise his religious duties, to safeguard him from corrupting influences and dangerous temptations and to ensure that he does not neglect his family or squander his earnings. He must also avoid asking the worker to toil beyond his physical strength, or to engage in work that is not suitable to his age and sex.

A just wage

His principal duty is to pay his workers what is demanded by justice. Many things have to be considered in order to determine what is a just wage but, in general, all capitalists and employers must remember that neither the divine nor the human law permits them to oppress the needy and the destitute for their own gain, or to traffic upon the misery of their fellow man. To defraud anyone of wages that are his due is a despicable crime that calls down the vengeance of heaven. *Behold the hire of the laborers . . . which by fraud has been kept back by you, crieth; and the cry of them hath entered into the ears of the Lord of Sabaoth* (James 5:4). Finally, the rich must refrain in conscience from any act of force, fraud or usury which would cause loss to the worker's savings. That duty becomes stronger when, due to his weakness and lack of protection, the slender savings the worker has set aside have become even more precious.

All must strive for eternal life

Would the observation of these laws not be sufficient in itself to dampen strife and take away the causes of dissension? But the Church, with Jesus Christ as her Master and Guide, looks even higher still because she wants to bring the two classes closer together, and to join them in the bonds of friendship. We are unable to understand and evaluate the things we see today unless we look beyond them to eternal life, without which the very idea of what is good and decent would perish, and the whole of creation would become an impenetrable mystery, beyond the ken of man. Therefore, that which we learn from nature itself, and which the Church has made its fundamental teaching as the basis of all religion, is the fact that we gain our true and eternal life when this life is over. God Himself has not created man for this passing and perishable life, but for a heavenly and eternal life, and He has given us the earth as a place of temporary exile, rather than as an everlasting homeland.

As for riches and such things, that men see as good and desirable, whether we have them or not is of no moment for eternal life, but it is their good or evil use that matters. The various trials and sorrows which are interwoven into our human lives were not taken away by Jesus Christ when He redeemed us with a *plentiful redemption*. What He did was to turn them into opportunities for the practice of virtue so that we may gain merit from them. It is a truth that no child of Adam can enter heaven unless he follows in the bloodstained footprints of his Redeemer. *If we suffer with Him, we shall also reign with Him* (IITim, 2: 12). When He took upon Himself labour and suffering, He thereby lessened the strength of our own labour and suffering. He did this not only by His example, but also by His grace, and by the hope held out for an eternal reward He has made suffering easier for us, *for that which is at present momentary and light of our tribulation, worketh for us above measure exceedingly an eternal weight of glory* (IICor. 4: 17).

Right use of riches

Therefore, those whom fortune favours are warned that riches do not take away sorrow, nor do they necessarily help towards eternal life but, rather, they can be an obstacle to it (Matt. 19: 23-24 ; Luke 6: 24-25). Indeed, the rich ought to fear the unusually severe threat of Jesus Christ who warns them that one day they will have to make an account to God of how they have used their riches. There is an excellent and important teaching on the use of riches which the ancient philosophers hinted at, but which the Church has brought to perfection, so much so that it is no longer a matter of mere speculation but one which must also guide men's lives. The basis of such a teaching rests on the distinction between the possession and the use of riches. As we have seen above, a natural right of man to own private property and to exercise this right, especially as a member of society, is not only lawful but also necessary. *It is lawful for a man to possess private property and it is also necessary to do so to sustain human life* (Thomas Aquinas, Summa Theol., 2a-2ae, Q. lxvi. art. 2). But, if it be further asked how should we use our possessions, the Church replies without hesitation that *'man should not hold his material possessions as if they were his own, but as common to all, so as to share them without hesitation when others are in need. Whence the Apostle says, 'command the rich of this world . . . to offer without stint, to apportion largely'.* (Ibid.).

It is certain that no one is obliged to come to the aid of others with that which is necessary for himself and those who belong to him, even of those things which he reasonably requires to maintain his state in life with dignity *'for no one ought to live other than becomingly'* (Ibid. Q. xxxii, art. 6). But, once he has satisfied his own needs in a manner befitting his state in life, he has a duty to help the needy with what he has over. *'Of that which remaineth giveth alms'* (Luke 11: 41). Except in the case of extreme necessity, it is true that this is not an obligation in justice, but of Christian charity, which cannot be demanded of anyone in a strictly legal sense. Nevertheless, above the laws and judgements of men, stand the law and judgement of Christ Who is God and Who, in so many ways, urges the practice of charity. 'It is more blessed to give than to receive' (Acts 20 : 35). He also held that what was done for, or denied to, the poor was done to, or denied to, Him. *'As long as you did it to one of My least brethren you did it to Me'.* (Matthew 25: 40)

To sum up, then, what has been said: whoever has received from the divine bounty a large share of temporal blessings, whether they be of the body, of material things, or of the soul, has received them to use for his own perfection, and at the same time, as a minister of divine providence for the good of others. *'He who has a human gift must see that he does not hide it. He who has an abundance of worldly goods must not be slow to share them with others. He who has art and skill must be quick to share the use and effects of them with his neighbour'* (St Gregory The Great, Hom. ix. in Evangel. n.7).

No shame in poverty and work

The Church teaches those who do not possess the gifts of fortune that, in the eyes of God, poverty is not a thing to be ashamed of, nor should they hang their heads because they are forced to earn their bread by work. Christ the Lord reinforced this fact by His own life because, for the salvation of men, *'whereas He was rich, He became poor for our sake'* (II Corinthians, 8: 9). Despite the fact that He was the Son of God and God Himself, He wanted to be thought of and seen as the son of a carpenter and He even went so far as not to refuse to pass the greater part of His life working as a carpenter. *'Is not this the carpenter, the son of Mary?* (Mark, 6: 3). By contemplating this divine example, it is more readily understood that the true dignity and greatness of man lie in his moral qualities, that is, in virtue; that virtue is truly the common inheritance of men, open both to the high and to the lowly, to the rich and to the workers and that only because of virtuous works, done by whomsoever, will the reward of everlasting happiness be reaped. Let us go a step further and say that it seems that God Himself has reserved a special love for the less fortunate and for the poor, whom Jesus Christ calls the blessed. [*Blessed are the poor in spirit.* Matt. 5:3] He lovingly invites those in labour and grief to come to Him for comfort. [*Come to Me all you that labour and are burdened and I will refresh you.* Ibid. 11: 8.]] He embraces with a special love those who are weak and who suffer injury.

Class conflict thereby eliminated

These truths ought to be especially useful in dampening the pride of the well-to-do and in giving heart to the unfortunate, by moving the former to be generous and the latter to be modest. Thus, the separation which pride tends to cause would start to disappear, nor would it any longer be difficult to ensure that the two classes, holding their hands out to each other, would come together in friendship.

If they obey the law of the Gospel, the two classes will not only be joined in a simple form of friendship but they will also want to embrace each other in brotherly love. For they will both feel and understand that each and every human being is the child of a common Father Who is God; that all have the same last end, God Himself, Who alone can bring both angels and men to perfect and absolute happiness; that all have been equally redeemed by Jesus Christ and called to the dignity of sons of God by Jesus Christ Who is *the first-born among many brethren* and with Whom they are joined in a blessed brotherhood. They will also know that the blessings of nature and of grace are the common possession of the human race and that no one, except the unworthy, will be disinherited from a place in the Kingdom of Heaven. *If sons, heirs also; heirs indeed of God, and co-heirs with Christ* (Romans 7: 17).

Such is the ideal form of duties and rights which is taught by the Christian ethic. If it prevailed in the world, would not all conflict cease immediately?

Example set by the Church

Therefore, the Church does not merely point out the way to a remedy, but she applies it herself with her maternal hand. For the whole striving of the Church is to teach and form men so that the healing waters of her doctrines may flow freely and, through the work of the bishops and the clergy, diffuse her teachings everywhere. At the same time, she strives to penetrate the minds and shape the wills of men, so that they may allow themselves to be governed by the divine precepts. It is exactly in this fundamental and momentous arena, upon which all else rests, that the Church alone can act with the highest power. The means which she uses to move souls were given to her by Jesus Christ and have in themselves a divine strength. Only they can penetrate into the intimate fibres of the heart and bring men to obey the voice of duty, restrain their passions, love with a supreme and singular love both God and neighbour and courageously break down all the obstacles that block them on the path of virtue.

It is enough to look to the past for clear examples which help to illustrate this point. Society was transformed from its base to its summit through the work of Christianity, and this transformation was a genuine form of progress for the human race. Indeed, it was a resurrection from death to life of such perfection that nothing like it had ever been known in the past, nor will be in the future. Jesus Christ was the cause and end of all these blessings because from Him they all came and to Him they return. Once the world had come to understand the great mystery of the Incarnation of the Word and the redemption of man through the light of the Gospels, the life of Jesus the God-man pervaded civil society and transformed it by His faith, precepts and laws.

Therefore, if the society of the human race is to be healed, it can only be through a return to Christian life and institutions. It is a solemn principle that, if a society is to be raised from decadence, it can only be through its return to the foundations from which it sprang. The perfection of every society is to work for and attain the end for which it was formed, since the generating principle of any movement or social act is the same as that which gave the society its beginning. Hence, to deviate from the original purpose brings corruption; to return to it brings healing. This is a great truth which applies to the whole of civil society, as it does in the same way to that portion of it, by far the majority, who earn their bread by work.

The Church cares about the earthly needs of the workers

Let it not be believed that the care of the Church is wholly and uniquely concerned with the salvation of souls, in such a way as to neglect earthly and mortal needs. She especially wants the workers to emerge from their depressed state and better their condition and, indeed, she strives for this. In no small way does she do this by calling men to virtue and forming them for its practice. Christian morality, where it is observed integrally, also contributes in itself to earthly prosperity for it calls down the blessing of God, Who is the source of all blessings, and it restrains the greed for possessions and the thirst for pleasure that are twin plagues which too often make a man miserable even in the midst of abundance. [*The desire for money is the root of all evil*. I Tim. 6: 10.] Christian morality makes a man happy with a frugal way of life when he sets aside savings for his future needs, and it keeps him free from vices which not only consume small fortunes but cast down in ruins even a large inheritance.

The Church, furthermore, works directly for the good of the workers by creating and promoting many institutions which she realises are useful for the relief of their poverty. In this respect, she has been so successful that she has won the praise even of her enemies. Among the early Christians, the strength of brotherly love was such that those with many possessions often deprived themselves of them in order to come to the aid of others so that '*neither was there any one needy amongst them* (Acts. 6: 34). The order of the diaconate was expressly instituted for this purpose by the Apostles, and the deacons were given the task of distributing charity daily while Paul, although burdened with the care of all the churches, did not hesitate to undertake tiresome voyages in order to distribute the offerings of the faithful to poorer Christians.

Tertullian calls the offerings, made spontaneously by the faithful in their meetings, *deposits of piety* which were employed *in feeding the needy, in burying them, in support of youths and young women destitute of means and deprived of their parents, in the care of the aged, and the relief of the shipwrecked* (Apologia Secunda, xxxix). In this way, over time, that patrimony came into being which the Church always guards with religious devotion because it is the inheritance of the poor. By its use, the poor were relieved of the shame of begging because the Church was able to come to their aid.

Christian charity is indispensable

Therefore, as the mother of the rich and of the poor, the Church aroused in all the heroism of charity, and created religious societies and many other useful, charitable institutions which did not leave in misery and destitution anyone who needed help and comfort. Today, there are many who, like the non-believers in former times, try to blame the Church for its high role in charity and they believe that it is better to substitute it with relief organised by the State. But there is no work of human ingenuity that can take the place of Christian charity, which is totally consecrated to the good of others. Christian charity is a virtue which cannot exist apart from the Church, because it rises from the most Sacred Heart of Christ. Whoever seeks to distance himself from the Church does so from Christ.

It is, nonetheless, true, that, to attain the result we are speaking of, all the means that are within human reach are required. It is necessary that all who have the problem of the workers at heart should be united and do their part towards the common end. In this, as with that providential order that governs the world, it is ordinarily the case that a good effect is produced by the harmonious co-operation of all the causes upon which it depends.

The role of the State

It is now appropriate to ask what role the State should play in this matter. We are not speaking of the State as it is constituted or functions in this or that nation. We speak of the State in its essence, as understood by right reason and in perfect harmony with Catholic doctrine, as we ourselves have expounded it in the encyclical letter *On the Christian Constitution of the State*. The first duty of the rulers of the State should be to ensure that the laws and political institutions generally work in such a way that the direction and administration of the State naturally results in public and private prosperity. This is the proper role of wise statemanship and it is the duty of the rulers of the people. The prosperity of the nations derives chiefly from the practice of true morality, properly conducted family life, respect for religion and justice, the moderate imposition and equal distribution of taxes, the progress of the arts, industry and commerce, the development of agriculture and similar matters which, to the degree that they are fostered, bring the people to a better and happier state of life.

By acting in this way, the rulers of the State thereby greatly contribute to the well-being of all classes, including the workers. They do it by virtue of their office and without opening themselves to being suspected of undue interference, since it is the province and competence of the State to serve the common good. To the extent that great good will come to all through this general way of acting, so much the less will it be necessary to take special means for the welfare of workers.

Equal rights of the workers

Furthermore, another thing has to be kept in mind that deeply affects this matter. The State is a harmonious whole which embraces equally the high and the low. Neither more nor less than the rich, the workers are citizens by a natural right; they are true and living members who, with their families, are part of the body of the commonwealth. It need hardly be added that, in every city, the workers make up the majority of the inhabitants. Since it would be absurd to provide for one section of the people and neglect the other, the public authorities must pay proper attention to safeguarding the wellbeing of the workers. Not to do so is to violate the law of justice, which demands that each shall have his due. On this question, Thomas Aquinas spoke wisely, *As the part and the whole are in a certain sense identical, so that which belongs to the whole in a sense belongs to the part* (Summa Theol., 2a-2ae, Q. lxi, art. 2). Therefore, among the many and grave duties that rulers have who want to do their best for their people, the chief one is to provide equally for every section of the community by acting with unshakeable impartiality towards all with that kind of justice which is called *distributive*.

The workers fundamental to every society

Although all the citizens, without exception, ought to contribute to the common good, which naturally reflects on the individual good, nonetheless, it is never the case that the contribution of each is either equal or the same. Irrespective of what changes the forms of government undergo, there will always be differences and inequalities, without which a human community cannot exist or even be thought of. It is clearly necessary in any State that there be rulers, legislators, judges and those who, by their advice and authority, direct the nation in peace and defend it in war.

It follows that such men are accepted as occupying the principal positions in the State, given that their work concerns most directly and effectively the common good of all. The workers are not able in the same way, and with the same effect, to promote the common good but, nonetheless, they also make a great, if less direct, contribution to it. Without doubt, the highest good that society can possess is virtue because its purpose is to better the condition of everyone. Nonetheless, in every well-ordered society there must be found a sufficient quantity of material goods, *the use of which is necessary to virtuous action* (Thomas Aquinas. On the Governance of Rulers. i. 15). In order that we may be provided with these goods, the labour and skill of workers is absolutely indispensable, whether they are engaged in agriculture or industry. Indeed, it is a manifest truth that their work is so essential that only through it can States grow wealthy.

Justice, therefore, demands that the public authorities ensure that the workers share in that which they themselves produce for the community, so that, provided with proper housing and other necessities, they may lead healthy lives in reasonable comfort. Whence it follows that anything that is done for the wellbeing of the workers must be fostered, in the certainty that whatever is done for them will be for the good of all, and cause no harm to anyone. Surely it is of general interest that those who contribute so greatly to society must not remain in misery.

Common good the supreme law

As we have said, the State is not permitted to swallow up either the individual or the family; it is right that each should be allowed that degree of freedom of action which is consistent with the common good and the rights of others. Nevertheless, whoever governs a society must take care of both the community and all its parts. The community must be fostered and protected because responsibility for it was committed by nature to the highest authority in such a way that the common good is not only the supreme law but the unique and absolute reason for the existence of the public authority. The various parts of the community must also be kept in mind because wisdom and Christian teaching agree that a government essentially exists for the good of those who are governed, rather than for the good of those who govern. Since the power to govern comes from God, and as such is a form of participation in His divine sovereignty, it must be used as He uses His, by which, with paternal care, He provides no less for the individual than for the whole.

Necessity of State intervention

Therefore, when either society as a whole or any of its parts suffer or are threatened with harm, the intervention of the State is necessary if the matter cannot be put right in any other way. Now, it is in the interest of the wellbeing of individuals as well as of the community, that good order and peace be maintained; that family life be lived in conformity with the law of God and nature; that religion should be observed and practised; that high levels of public and private morality be maintained; that justice be regarded as sacred; that no group of citizens oppress another group and that the citizens may grow up healthy and strong, ready to help and to defend their country if necessary.

Whence it follows that if, through a strike by workers, or by concerted interruption of work, public disorder is feared; if among the workers, natural family relationships should be substantially relaxed; if the religious duties of the workers are not respected because they are denied convenient and sufficient time to carry them out; if, through promiscuity, between the sexes and through other dangerous occasions of sin in workplaces, harm is being done to morality; if the workers are oppressed by employers laying unjust burdens on them, or they are degraded by conditions repugnant to their human dignity and personality; if by excessive labour, or by work not suited to their sex and age, harm is done to the health of the workers, in all these instances the power and the authority of the State should be used within proper limits. The limits are determined by the reason which moves the State to intervene, which means that the law must not go beyond what is required to repair the evil or to remove the danger.

Weak and needy have special claims

Rights, wherever they exist, must be religiously respected and it is the duty of the public authority to assure to each his rights by preventing and punishing injury done to anyone. Nonetheless, when it is a question of defending the rights of individuals, the weak and the needy have a claim to special consideration. Those who are wealthy have their own power and thereby have less need of public protection, whereas the mass of the poor, who lack resources of their own, rely especially on the State for assistance. It is for this reason that the workers, since they are numbered among the needy, should by preference be given the care and protection of the State.

State must safeguard private property

At this stage, it is useful to come to some particular matters of great importance. The chief one is that it is the duty of public authority to safeguard private property by the power and strength of law. It is absolutely necessary that people stand by their duties in a time noted for so much unbridled greed because, if it is just for everyone to try to better their condition of life, neither justice nor the common good allows anyone to take that which belongs to another nor, under the pretext of an absurd claim to equality, to violate the possessions of others. It is unquestionably the case that the vast majority of the workers want to better themselves by honest labour, without doing harm to others. Nonetheless, there are not a few who have been swayed by false principles and, burning with the desire for change, they try at any cost to stir up the masses and move them to violence. The authority of the State must intervene to rein in such agitators, and, thereby, preserve the decent workers from being corrupted by their wiles as well as protect legitimate owners from despoliation.

Strikes

Overprolonged hours of work, too heavy labour and the fact that they consider their wages to be too low, often give the workers a motive to go out on strike, during which time they are voluntarily idle. Public authority should mediate to prevent such grave and frequent occurrences, because strikes affect not only the owners and the workers themselves, but also commerce and the public interest. Furthermore, such occasions often give rise to violence and disorder and frequently put public tranquillity at risk. The best and safest remedy in such cases is to use the authority and influence of the State to forestall and prevent their happening, by removing in good time the causes which give rise to conflict between the owners and the workers.

Right to eternal life is universal

Likewise, there are many areas in which the worker must be protected by the State and the first is the good of his soul. Earthly life, however good and desirable, is not the end in itself for which we are born. It is merely the way and means to bring our spiritual life to perfection by the knowledge of the truth and the love of the good. The image and likeness of God is sculptured in the soul and therein resides that sovereignty by virtue of which man is ordered to rule over inferior creatures and to make the whole earth and the oceans useful to him. *Fill the earth and subdue it; and rule over the fishes of the sea, and the fowls of the air, and all living creatures that move upon the earth* (Gen. I:

28). In this matter, all men are equal, nor is there the slightest difference between rich and poor, masters and servants, monarchs and subjects *for the same is Lord over all* (Rom. X: 12).

The fundamental principle of all social justice

No one may outrage with impunity that human dignity which God Himself treats *with great reverence*, or impede in any way that striving for perfection which is consistent with eternal life. Moreover, man himself can never renounce his right to be treated according to his nature or to surrender himself to any form of slavery of the spirit. In this matter is is not a question of rights which a man is free to renounce, but of duties towards God which must be held as sacred.

Right to Sunday rest

From this flows the need to cease work on Sundays and feast days. Such rest is not to be understood as mere idleness or, as many would want it, a chance to engage in vice and to squander money. It is rather to be seen as a time consecrated by religion. Once joined to religion, such rest takes a man away from his toils and his day-to-day affairs, so that he may turn his mind to the things of heaven and to the worship he so rightly owes to the Godhead. In this, principally, we understand the nature and purpose for resting on Sundays and feast days, a rest which God prescribed for man with a special law in the Old Testament when He said, *Remember to keep holy the Sabbath day* (Exod XX: 8), and which He taught us by example when, immediately after creating man, He rested in a mysterious way. *He rested on the seventh day from all His work which He had done* (Gen. II: 2).

Conditions of work

Insofar as bodily and material wants are concerned, the first duty is to save the suffering workers from the cruelty of wealthy tycoons, who use human beings as mere instruments to increase their capital. It is neither just nor humane to demand such a quantity of work from a man that his mind is stupefied and his body worn out. There are bounds beyond which a man cannot go because his strength, like his nature, is limited. His strength is developed by use and exercise provided, however, that he rests in order to recover from his labour.

Work, therefore, should never go beyond that certain number of hours which strength permits. The length of periods of rest should depend on the kind of work done, on the time and the place and on the health and strength of the worker. For example, work done in quarries when extracting stone, iron and metals from the bowels of the earth, because it is more strenuous and more injurious to health, should be compensated for by shorter working hours. Regard too must be had to the season, because it is often the case that work done in one season is easily undertaken, while at another time of the year it is impossible, or cannot be engaged in without great difficulty.

Women and children workers

Finally, it is never reasonable to ask the same work of a woman or of a child that is asked of a healthy, adult male. Insofar as children are concerned, they should not be allowed to start working in factories before an age at which their physical, intellectual and moral powers are sufficiently developed. Those developments which, in childhood, are like the buds of spring, are destroyed by too precocious a growth and make the education of the child impossible. A woman is less adapted for certain kinds of work because she is formed by nature for domestic tasks, best suited to protect her true status and corresponding naturally to the bringing up of the children and the wellbeing of the household.

The work contract

In this matter, the general guide to be followed is that the amount of rest necessary for the worker should be in proportion to the amount of strength he uses up in his work, because what is used up must be restored by rest. In every agreement made between the employers and the workers there is always an express or tacit understanding of a period of rest for soul and body. Were this not the case the agreement would be immoral, because it is wrong to demand from the one side, or offer from the other, the neglect of those duties which a man owes to God or to himself.

Let us now come to a matter of great importance which must be understood properly if extremes from either side are to be avoided. It is said that a wage is regulated by free consent so that the employer, once he has paid the wage agreed to, has done all required of him and owes nothing further. It would flow that an injustice would be involved only when the employer failed to pay the whole wage, or if the worker failed to do the work agreed to. As a consequence it is said that, in such circumstances, and only in those, is it right for the State to intervene in order that the rights of each party be preserved intact.

Dual nature of work

A fair-minded person would neither easily nor totally agree with this line of argument, because it does not look at the question from all sides and there are weighty considerations which it entirely neglects. Work is a human activity which has as its goal the provision of the necessities of life and, especially, its preservation. *In the sweat of thy face thou shalt eat bread* (Gen. III: 19). Consequently, human labour has two qualities which are impressed on it by nature. The first is *personal* because the power to work is bound up with the person, to whom it totally belongs and to whom it was given for his own advantage. Secondly, it is *necessary* because, without the fruits of his labour, a man cannot live and nature itself strictly commands that a man do all he can to preserve his life.

Were we to look at work only from the personal side, it is clear that the worker can agree to a low wage because, since he offers his labour voluntarily he can, if he wishes, be content with a low wage or, indeed, none at all. But we would come to an entirely different conclusion were we to consider both the *personal* and *necessary* aspects of work because they cannot be separated from each other. The preservation of life is a bounden duty which no one can neglect without grave fault. From this arises the necessary consequence of a right to procure the means to live which, in the case of the poor worker comes down to the wage he is paid for his work. Let the worker and the employer freely enter into an agreement on this matter and give their consent to a specified wage.

A living wage

Nonetheless, there is always an element of natural justice which is more ancient and higher than the free consent of the contracting parties; namely that a wage ought to be sufficient to support a frugal and well-behaved worker. Thus, if through necessity or fear of a worse fate, the worker is forced to accept a harsh agreement imposed by an employer or contractor, he is subject to a form of violence against which justice must protest. In this and similar cases, such as the hours of work in different trades and the health regulations to be observed in factories, lest the State interfere unduly, especially as circumstances, times and places differ so widely, it is wiser to reserve judgement to boards, about which we shall speak later on, or to some other way of safeguarding justly the interests of the workers, with the State only giving its sanction and support when the case so requires.

When a worker receives a wage sufficient to support himself and his wife and children in moderate comfort, if he is wise, he will find it easy to be thrifty. Acting on a natural impulse, he will ensure that, over and above his expenses, he will set something aside and thus secure a small piece of property because, as we have already shown, the inviolable right to private property is sacred and, furthermore, indispensable to the solution of the worker question. Therefore, the law should favour this right and, insofar as it can, act in such a way as to increase the number of property owners as much as possible.

Fruits of a living wage

From this many excellent results would follow and the first would certainly be a more equal distribution of wealth. The prevalence of civil disorder has divided the urban masses into two classes, between which it has carved an abyss. On the one side stand the most powerful group because they are rich. They control labour and trade, use for their own benefit and ends all the sources of riches and even have a strong influence on the administration of the State.

Standing on the other side is that needy and weak multitude of the people, wounded in spirit and thus often ready for disorder. Were it possible to encourage those people to be industrious so that they could hope to acquire some of the wealth of the land, little by little, the two groups would come closer together with the removal of the immense gap between great poverty and great wealth.

Moreover, a greater abundance of produce from the earth itself would result. When men know they are working their own land they toil harder and more readily; they learn to love the land they till with their own hands, land which gives forth not only the food they need but an abundance for themselves and those who belong to them. Anyone can see that such a spirit of willing labour would greatly help to increase the produce of the earth and the wealth of the nation. Another advantage would flow from this in that men would cling happily to the place in which they were born, nor would they want to exchange their native land for another if their own gave them the chance to live a decent life.

Unjust taxes

It is, however, impossible to achieve these several benefits unless on the condition that private means are not exhausted by the need to pay excessive taxes. The right to own private property does not flow from the law of man but from that of nature. Public authority cannot abolish that right, but can only moderate its use and harmonise it with the common good.

Therefore, the State would act in an unjust and inhumane manner were it to exact more than is just from private owners under the guise of a tax.

Helpful institutions

Finally, both the owners and the workers can make a great contribution to the resolution of the worker question by institutions set up to give aid when needed to those in distress, and to bring both groups more closely together. Such institutions are mutual benefit societies; the various private insurance bodies which provide for the worker, his widow and his orphans in cases of unforeseen calamity, in sickness and in other instances of human misfortune; and institutions for the welfare of boys and girls, for young people and for adults.

Trade unions foremost

The foremost place amongst such institutions is held by trade unions and they virtually include all the rest. Our ancestors were fully aware of the great good done by the ancient guilds. They benefited not only the workers, but they also honoured and perfected the arts they practised, and a great number of monuments survive to bear witness to that fact. Assuredly, the progress of education, the change in customs, and the increasing demands of daily life have made it necessary for such bodies to adapt to present conditions. We see with pleasure the formation everywhere of such associations, whether made up of workers alone or of workers and employers, and it is desirable that they increase in number and grow stronger. Although it is true that we have spoken of them more than once, we are pleased to treat of them now so as to explain how notably they are needed, to show that they have their own legitimate standing, and to examine how they should be organised and operated.

Public and private institutions

The consciousness of his own weakness moves man to want to unite his efforts with those of others. Sacred Scripture says, *It is better that two should be together than one; for they have the advantage of their society. If one fall he shall be supported by the other. Woe to him that is alone, for when he falleth he hath none to lift him up* (Eccles. 4: 9-10). And further, *A brother that is helped by his brother is like a strong city* (Prov. 18: 19). This natural instinct moves men to join together in civil society, just as it moves them to unite with others in societies which, although they are small and not perfect, are nonetheless real societies. There is a distinct difference between civil society and such lesser bodies, given the ends they serve. The purpose of civil society is universal since it serves the common good, to a share in which each and every citizen has a right in due proportion. For that reason, it is called *public* because through it *men establish relations in common with each other in setting up a State* (Thomas Aquinas. Contra Impugnantes Dei Cultum et Religionem II).

On the contrary, those other societies which arise in the bosom of the State are called, and are, in fact, private because they have as their purpose the private advantage of their members. *A private society, however, is one which is formed for the purpose of carrying out private objects; as when two or three enter into partnership with the view of trading in commerce* (Ibid). Now, although such private societies exist within the State and are part of it, nevertheless, they cannot be absolutely, and in themselves, forbidden to exist by the State.

Right to form private institutions

It is the natural right of man to enter into such societies and the State has to protect the natural rights of its citizens, not to destroy them. By forbidding such societies, the State would contradict itself, for both it and they exist as a result of one and the same principle, namely, the natural tendency of man to dwell in society. It happens, at times, that the State has to forbid such societies as, for example, when they propose aims that are clearly bad, are against justice or are dangerous to the safety of the State. In such cases, public authority has the right to prevent such societies being formed or, if formed, to dissolve them. It is, however, necessary, to proceed with great caution in such matters so as not to infringe the rights of the citizens and not to impose unreasonable regulations under the pretext of the common good. For laws are only to be obeyed when they are in harmony with right reason and, hence, in accordance with the eternal law of God. [*Human law is law insofar as it accords with right reason and thus it becomes clear that it flows from the eternal law. To the extent that it departs from right reason, it is not law at all, but rather a kind of violence* (Thomas Aquinas. Summa Theol. 1a-2ae, Q. xciii. art. 3. ad. 2.)]

Rights of ecclesiastical foundations

Here, we are reminded of the societies, confraternities and religious orders of all kinds that have arisen with the authority of the Church, and through the piety of the faithful. Right into our own day, history tells us how much good they have done for the human race. Such bodies, when considered only in the light of reason and given that they have blameless objectives, are clearly legitimate by natural right. Insofar as their religious purposes are concerned, they are not subject to any authority but that of the Church. The State, therefore, cannot claim any authority over them, nor can it take from them the right to administer their own affairs. On the contrary, it has the duty to respect them, to cherish them, and, when necessary, defend them.

How far from that state of things are we, especially in our own times? In many places and in many ways the State has placed such societies under the control of the civil law, taken away their rights as corporate bodies and despoiled them of their property. The Church has her own rights in such property and each member of those bodies has his or her own rights, as also do those who set them up and those to whose advantage and for whose assistance they were established. As a consequence, we cannot refrain from deploring such despoliation, which is so unjust and harmful. We do so with all the more reason because, concurrently with the law proclaiming freedom of association for all, we see that Catholic associations are obstructed in every way, irrespective of their tranquillity and usefulness. At the same time, such a right of association is widely granted to men who are openly sworn to destroy religion and harm the State itself.

Dangerous associations

Today, far more than before, there are associations of every kind and, especially, among the workers. It is not our place here to enquire of these what their origins are, what are their objects or the means they use. However, based on firm evidence, many hold that some of them are often led by secret leaders and that they are organised in a way contrary to Christian principles and public wellbeing and that, having monopolised organised labour, they make those who refuse to join them pay dearly. In such a state of affairs, Christian workers have only two options. They can either join such associations with peril to their faith, or set up Christian associations themselves, and thus unite their forces in order to shake off with courage such unjust and intolerable oppression. How can there be any hesitation about choosing the latter path by anyone who does not wish to imperil man's chief good?

Catholic associations

There are many Catholics worthy of the highest praise who, aware of the needs of the day, do all they can to use right means in order to better the conditions of the workers. They have taken the cause in hand by trying to increase individual and domestic wellbeing, by regulating with justice the relations between employers and workers and by inculcating in both an awareness of the demands of duty and the precepts of the Gospels. Those precepts are the very ones which cause a man to be moderate and turn from all forms of excess, and they, thereby, help to maintain harmony among the wide range of persons and interests that make up civil society. We have witnessed distinguished men meeting in Congresses to that end, at which they have communicated their ideas to each other. Others strive to group together various kinds of workers, help them with their advice and other forms of assistance, and see that they do not lack honest and profitable employment. The bishops readily give them their own good will and support and, with their authority and guidance, many of both the religious and secular clergy work hard for the spiritual good of the members of such associations.

Finally, there are many well-off Catholics who have made common cause with the workers and who have spent large sums to found and foster in many places bodies that help the worker, not only to provide by his labour for his present needs, but also to assure for himself an honourable and tranquil retirement in the future. The benefits that such multiple and willing activities have brought to the community at large are so well-known that they need not be dealt with here. On this account, we have great hope for the future, provided the associations we have spoken of flourish more widely and are well and wisely administered. The State should defend these legitimate associations of its citizens, but it should not intrude into their private manner of conducting their affairs. Things live and move by the spirit which motivates them, and undue interference from without can suffocate that spirit.

Qualities of good organisations

Wise forms of organisations and control are absolutely necessary in order that there be unity and purpose in any association. If citizens have, in fact as well as principle, the freedom and right to join together in an association, they must have, likewise, the equal right to choose for their members the appropriate rules and forms of organisation they think will best serve their ends.

We do not regard it as possible to define with clear and precise rules the way any particular association ought to be governed, since such matters are best determined by national characteristics, by experience and practice, by the mode and method of production, by the development of commerce, as well as from other circumstances which must be prudently considered according to the time and place. Nonetheless, to sum up, it can be said firmly that there is a general and constant law by which workers' associations are to be organised and governed. It is that they must offer to their members the most apt and proper means to attain the ends they strive for. Those ends are set down to help every individual member achieve, as far as possible, the good of his body, soul and property.

It is clear that such associations must have as their principal goal the religious and moral perfection of their members and that all social betterment has this as its aim. Otherwise, they would degenerate and end up as little different from those other kinds of associations which have no truck with religion. What use is it to a worker to gain from a society a degree of material wellbeing if his soul is endangered by a lack of spiritual food. *What doth it profit a man, if he gain the whole world and suffer the loss of his soul?* (Matt. 16: 26). According to the teaching of Christ the Lord, the very characteristic which distinguishes the non-believer from the Christian is contained in the words, *After all these things do the non-believers seek . . . Seek ye first the Kingdom of God and His justice: and all these things shall be added unto you.* (Ibid. 6: 32, 33).

Acting on this principle, which comes from God, let religious instruction have a leading role so that each member may have a knowledge of his duty to God, know well what he must believe, hope in and do for eternal life and let all be forewarned against false teachings and corrupting principles. Let the worker be drawn to the worship of God and the earnest practice of religion, and, especially, to the observance of Sundays and the feast days of the Church. Let him learn to revere and love the Church, the common Mother of us all, to obey her precepts and receive the sacraments, which are the divine means of justification and holiness.

Rights and duties

Once the foundations of the association are based on religion, it is open to us to establish guidelines governing the relations of the members to each other in order that they may work together in peace and prosperity. The responsibilities of the members should be proportionate to the common aim, and shared in such a way that differences in rank do not prejudice unity. It is of the utmost importance that office-bearers be appointed wisely, and their duties clearly set down, so that no member may feel aggrieved. The common funds and possessions must be administered with integrity, so that each member may receive assistance in proportion to his needs. The rights and duties of the employer must be in harmony with those of the worker. When either thinks that he has suffered injury in any way, nothing would be better than that a board, made up of upright and competent members of the association be formed, to the judgement of which, in conformity with the rules of the association, he would submit himself.

A foremost responsibility of the association should be to ensure that no worker lacks employment at any time, as well as to have a source of funds from which the members may be helped when in need; not only on account of sudden and accidental crises in industry, but also when the workers are afflicted by illness, old age or any other misfortune.

When such rules and regulations are voluntarily embraced they will be sufficient to ensure the wellbeing of the less fortunate and Catholic associations, especially, are certain to contribute in no small degree to the prosperity of the State.

Example of the past

With good reason we are able to look into the future based on the experience of the past. One century gives way to another, so that the events of one are wonderfully like those of another because they are all governed by the providence of God, which directs and turns the course of history to the end for which the human race was created.

In the early days of the Church, the Christians were reproached because most of them had to live by begging or working. Nonetheless, poor and weak, they managed to win the sympathy of the rich and the protection of the powerful. They showed themselves as industrious, hard-working and peaceful and they gave a shining example of justice and love for each other. By the spectacle of such a way of life, and through the force of their example, they caused prejudice against them to vanish, malevolent tongues were muted and the lying legends of ancient superstition gave way gradually to Christian truth.

Worker question must be solved

The most pressing problem of our day is the worker question and its solution is of great concern to the wellbeing of the State. Christian workers will solve it properly if, united in associations and wisely led, they follow the way trodden, with such great advantage to themselves and society, by their fathers before them. Prejudice and the love of money are certainly powerful forces working on men, nevertheless, if the sense of what is just and right be not deliberately stifled, such men will not be able to avoid a feeling of goodwill towards the workers when they see how hard they toil, how moderate they are, and how they put honesty before the love of money and the conscientious following of duty before all else.

Another great advantage would likely follow with the hope and indeed security that those workers who have lost the faith would find it awakened again, and those who have fallen away from following its precepts would return to the practice of them. In most cases, they know that they have been fooled by false hopes and vain illusions. They feel that their greedy employers have treated them with gross inhumanity, and that they are valued less than the goods which, for the profit of the same employers, they toil to produce. They also know that among their fellow workers, with whom they have been caught up, instead of charity and love, there is often internal discord, which is the handmaiden of the kind of poverty that lacks patience and faith.

Broken in spirit and worn down in body, how greatly do so many of them long to be released from the yoke of such abject slavery? But they do not dare to break their bonds for fear of what others would think of them, or because they face starvation if they do so. The Catholic associations would solve the problems of so many of these workers and bring great benefits to them. They would do so by holding out their arms to the workers as they stand hesitant to join and, once within their embrace and under their protection, the workers would become conscious again of their great dignity.

Appeal to bishops and clergy

You now have before you, Venerable Brothers, a description of both the persons and the means through which this difficult matter of the worker question must be solved. Everyone must do his allotted task without delay, because to vacillate now could render incurable an evil which is already so great. Those who hold authority in the State must use its laws and institutions; wealthy owners and employers must be ever-conscious of their duty and the workers, whose interests are most at stake in this matter, should do all they can within the limits of justice. Since, as we have said from the start, no true and radical solution can be found unless it is based in religion, everyone should be persuaded of the necessity of following a Christian way of life, without which all the strategies seen as most suitable will fall short of the mark.

Insofar as the Church is concerned, she will never be lacking in doing all she can, and in whatever way possible, to help solve the worker question. Her actions will prove ever more beneficial, the more she is free to act. That fact must be always in the minds of those responsible for the wellbeing of the State. Ministers of religion, calling upon the strength of their courageous spirits and the generosity of their zeal, must do all they can in this matter. Guided by your authority and example, Venerable Brothers, they will never tire of inculcating among all sections of society the life-giving precepts of the Gospels; they will do all they can for the salvation of the people and, above all, they will foster in themselves and awaken in others, the high and the lowly, the virtue of charity which is mistress and queen of all the virtues.

Christian charity paramount

In conclusion, the desired effect which we all long for will principally come from a great outpouring of charity. We mean Christian charity, which contains in itself the whole law of the Gospels, which is always ready to sacrifice itself for the good of others and is the safest antidote that man can use against worldly pride and immoderate love of self. The essence of Christian charity, as well as its divine features, are expressed by the Apostle Paul in these words, *Charity is patient, is kind . . . seeketh not her own . . . suffereth all things . . . endureth all things* (I Cor. 13: 4-7).

Leo's blessing on all

Venerable Brothers, as a promise of God's heavenly gifts and as a mark of our warmth towards you, we give to each of you, ever lovingly in the Lord, our Apostolic blessing, as well as to your clergy and to your people.

Given at St Peter's, Rome, on 15 May 1891 in the fourteenth year of our Pontificate.

LEO PP. XIII

Index